RECORDED VERSIONS

GUITAR

AUTHENTIC TRANSCRIPTIONS
WITH NOTES AND TABLATURE

**Transcribed by
JEFF JACOBSON
PAUL PAPPAS**

AEROSMITH

GET A GRIP

C000253684

Photos: William Hames

Hal Leonard Publishing Corporation

7777 West Bluemound Road P.O. Box 13819 Milwaukee, WI 53213

Intro

By Steven Tyler

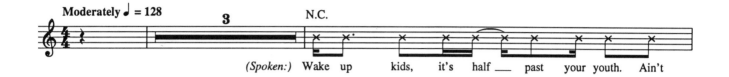

(Spoken:) Wake up kids, it's half __ past your youth. Ain't

noth- in' real- ly chang- in' but the date. You're a grand slam- mer, but you're no Babe Ruth.__ You got- ta

learn how to re - late or you'll be swing- in' from the pearl- y gate. __ I

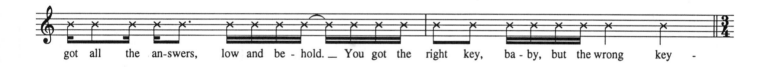

got all the an- swers, low and be - hold. __ You got the right key, ba - by, but the wrong key -

Segue to EAT THE RICH

hole, yo.

*Sampling effect arr. for gtr.

Eat The Rich

Words and Music by Steven Tyler, Joe Perry and Jim Vallance

*2nd time, and when Rhy. Fig. 1 is recalled, note is picked, not hammered.

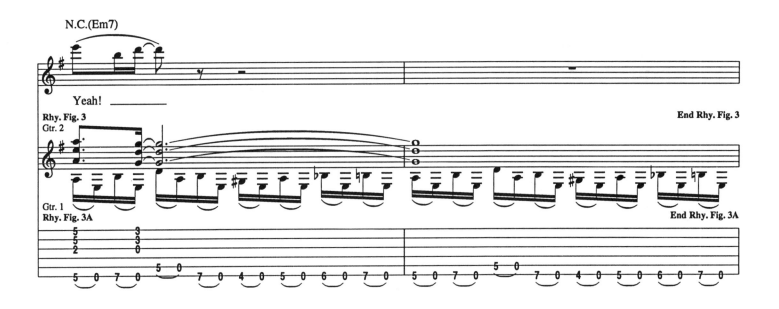

N.C.(Em7)

Yeah! _____

Rhy. Fig. 3
Gtr. 2

End Rhy. Fig. 3

Gtr. 1
Rhy. Fig. 3A

End Rhy. Fig. 3A

Verse

Gtr. 2: w/Rhy. Fig. 3
Gtr. 1: w/Rhy. Fig. 3A

Gtr. 2: w/Rhy. Fig. 3, (4 times)
Gtr. 1: w/Rhy, Fig. 3A, (4 times, 2nd time sustitute Rhy. Fill 2)

N.C.(Em7)

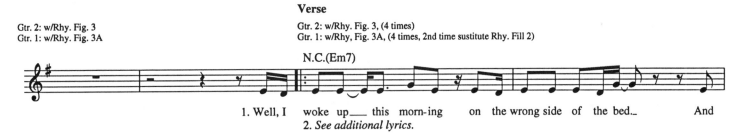

1. Well, I woke up___ this morn-ing on the wrong side of the bed.___ And
2. *See additional lyrics.*

how I got to think-in' a-bout-a all those things you said. ___ A-bout

or-di-nar-y peo-ple, and how they make you sick.___ And if

call-in' names___ kicks back on you,___ then I hope this does the trick. Cause I'm

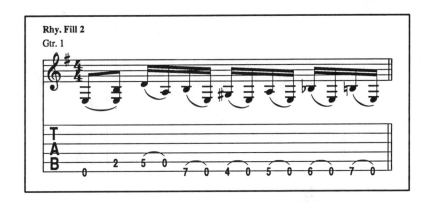

Rhy. Fill 2
Gtr. 1

Pre-chorus

Gtr. 2: w/Riff A

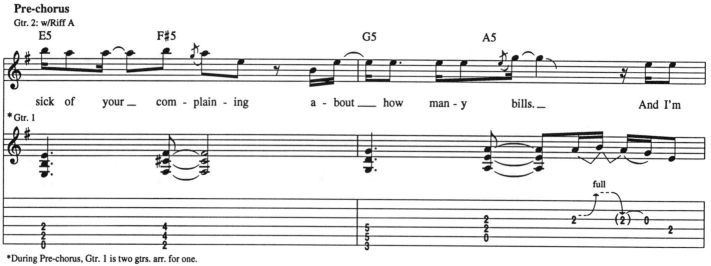

sick of your _ com-plain-ing a-bout _ how man-y bills. _ And I'm

*Gtr. 1

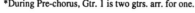

*During Pre-chorus, Gtr. 1 is two gtrs. arr. for one.

sick of all _ your bitch-in' 'bout your poo-dles and your pills. And I just can't see no hu-mor a-bout _

Gtr. 1: 2nd time w/ Rhy. Fill 3

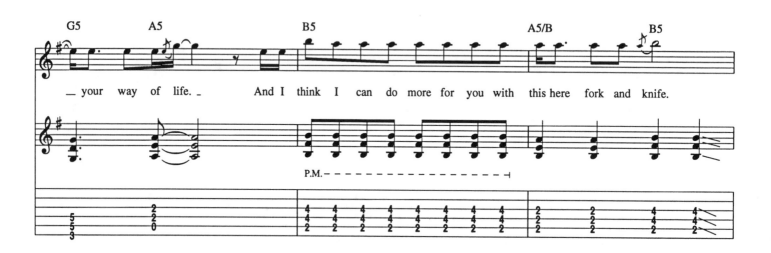

_ your way of life. _ And I think I can do more for you with this here fork and knife.

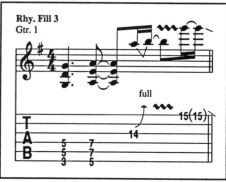

6

§ **Chorus**

Gtr. 1 & 2: w/Rhy. Fig. 4

Eat the __ rich, __ there's on-ly one thing that they're __ good for.

*Riff B
Gtr. 3

*Rhythms indicated are played 1st time only. All subsequent
appearances of Riff B are simile w/rhythmic variations ad lib.

Eat the _ rich, __ take-a one bite now, come back for more. __ Eat the _ rich, __ I

Gtr. 1: w/Rhy. Fill 1, (1st time)

To Coda ⊕

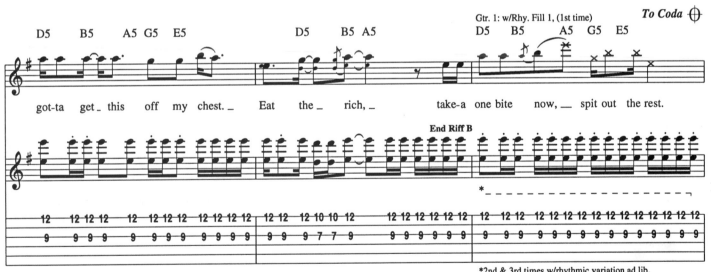

got-ta get _ this off my chest. __ Eat the _ rich, _ take-a one bite now, __ spit out the rest.

End Riff B

*2nd & 3rd times w/rhythmic variation ad lib.

Rhy. Fig. 4
Gtrs. 1 & 2

Play 4 times

Rhy. Fill 1
Gtr. 1

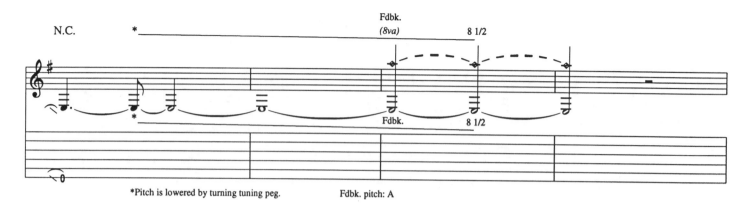

*Pitch is lowered by turning tuning peg.   Fdbk. pitch: A

Pre-chorus
Gtr. 2: w/Riff A

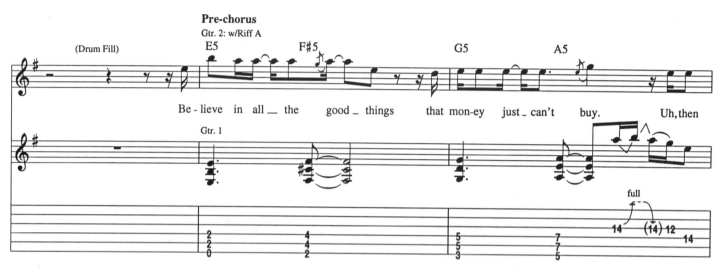

Be - lieve in all __ the good __ things that mon-ey just __ can't buy. Uh, then

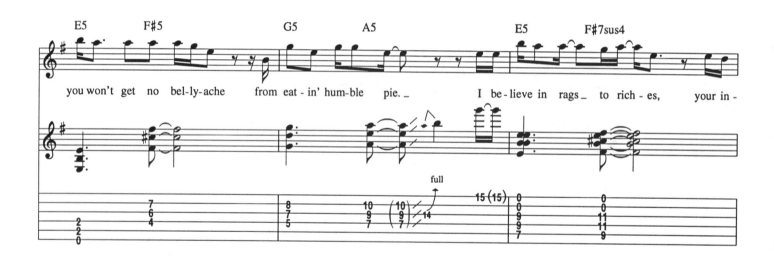

you won't get no bel-ly-ache from eat-in' hum-ble pie. __ I be-lieve in rags __ to rich-es, your in -

D.S. al Coda

her - i - tance won't last, so take your Grey Pou-pon, my friend, and __ shove it up your ass!

⊕ Coda

Outro

Gtr. 1 & 2: w/Rhy. Fig. 4, (1st 7 bars only)
Gtr. 3: w/Riff B
Gtr. 4: w/Riff C

Eat the ___ rich, ___ there's on-ly one thing that they're ___ good for.

Eat the ___ rich, ___ take-a one bite now, come back for more. ___

Eat the ___ rich, ___ don't stop me now, ___ I'm go-in' cra - zy.

Gtrs. 1 & 2: w/Rhy. Fill 5
Gtr. 3: w/Rhy. Fill 2

Eat the ___ rich, ___ that's my i - dea ___ of a good time, ba - by!

Additional Lyrics:

2. So I called up my head shrinker
   And I told him what I'd done.
   He said, "You'd best go on a diet,
   Yeah, I hope you have some fun.
   And-a don't go burst a bubble
   On the rich folks who get rude.
   'Cause you won't get in no trouble
   When you eats that kinda food."

2nd Pre-chorus:
Now they're smokin' up their junk bonds,
And then they go get stiff.
And they're dancin' at the yacht club
With Muff and Uncle Biff.
But there's one good thing that happens
When you toss your pearls to swine.
Their attitudes may taste like shit,
But go real good with wine.
(To Chorus:)

Get A Grip

Words and Music by Steven Tyler, Joe Perry and Jim Vallance

Gtr. 1: w/Rhy. Fig. 1
Gtr. 2: w/Rhy. Fig. 1A

Skin and bones, it ain't such a pit-y. Don't ya gim-me no flack, hon-ey, shut ya lip. Ya

3rd time to Coda II ⊕ Gtr. 1: w/Rhy. Fill 2, 3rd time   *2nd time to Coda I* ⊕

got-ta have stones if you're liv-in' in the cit-y. If ya wan-na hang loose, got-ta get a grip, rip.

Verse
N.C. (E5)

1. Once up-on a crime, I thought I

was cool, but I don't want to brag. __

14

Fever

Words and Music by Steven Tyler and Joe Perry

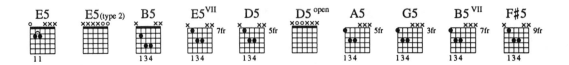

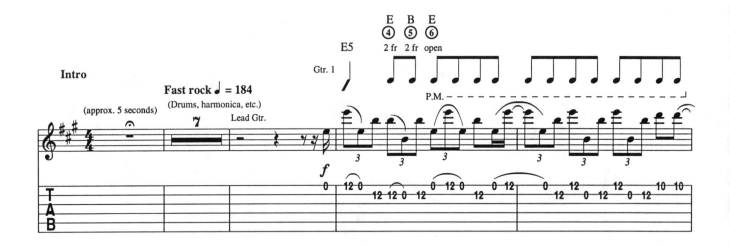

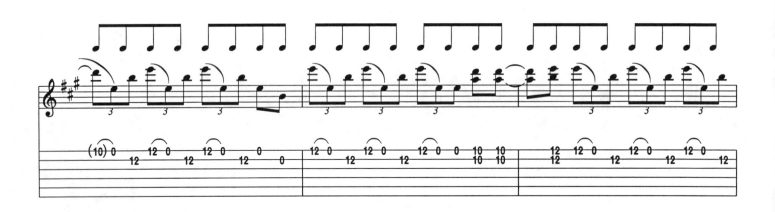

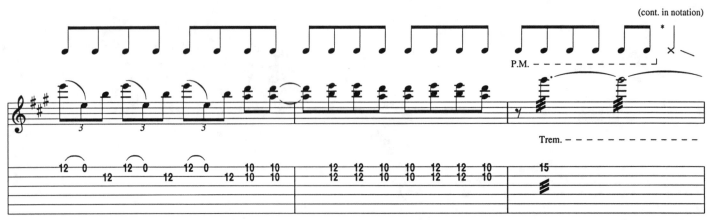

* Slide doubled by Gtr. II

1. I got a rip in my pants and a

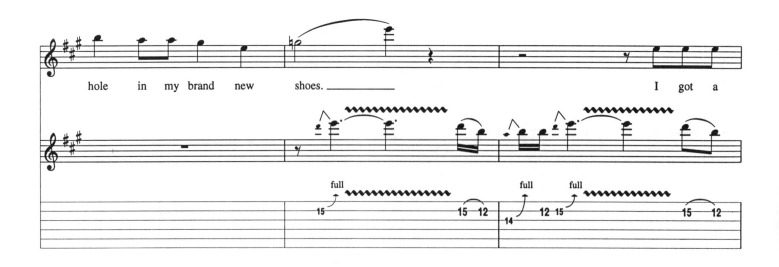

hole in my brand new shoes. _____ I got a

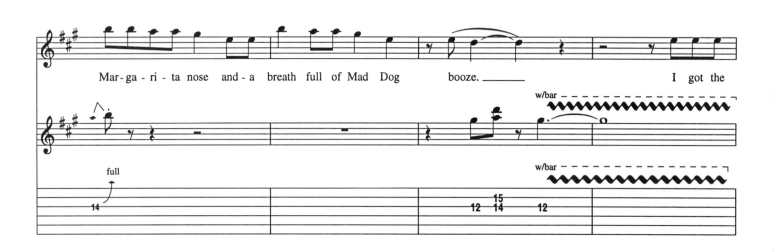

Mar - ga - ri - ta nose and - a breath full of Mad Dog booze. _____ I got the

Chorus

fe - ver, _____ fe - ver, _____

Gtr. 1

Gtr. 2

fe - ver, _____ fe - ver. _____ Yeah, they

(cont. in slashes)

full full full full

1/4

(cont. in slashes)

1/2

1/4

E
⑥
open E5 (type 2) G
⑥
3 fr B5 G
⑥
3 fr E
⑥
open E5 (type 2) G
⑥
3 fr B5 G
⑥
3 fr

Rhy. Fig. 3

Gtrs. 1 & 2

threw me out - ta jail, I tell ya it ain't fair. __ I tried to kiss the judge from the e - lec - tr - ic - a chair. Yeah,

E
⑥
open E5 (type 2) G
⑥
3 fr B5 E5 VII *D5

End Rhy. Fig. 3

Gtrs. 1 & 2: w/Rhy. Fig. 1 (2 times)
Lead Gtr.: w/Fill 1

N.C.

we're all here __ 'cause we're not all there __ to - night.

* Gtr. 2: substitute D5 open

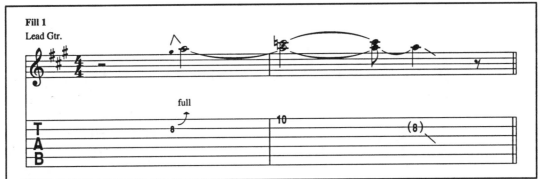

Fill 1
Lead Gtr.

full

10 (8)

Verse

Gtrs. 1 & 2: w/Rhy. Fig. 2, (4 times)

(Lead gtr. tacet)

N.C.

2. The gui-tar's cranked and the bass-man's blown a fuse. __ Hee,

hee. And when the whole gang bangs, tell me then what's your ex - cuse. _____ We got the

Chorus

E5

A5

fe - ver, _____ fe - ver, _____

Gtr. 1

let ring

full

full full full

Gtr. 2

1/2

1/4

let ring

1/4

fe - ver, _____ fe - ver. _____ Fe -

1/2

full

full

full

1/2

1/4

1/4

first - time - ev - er lov - er, we fell a - sleep out on the lawn. ___ And when

Gtr. 1: w/Rhy. Fig. 4
Gtr. 2: w/Rhy. Fig. 4A

I woke up I was all a - lone,__ mak-in' love to the crack of dawn. __ So, _ yo, ___ I beg yo par-

(Gtr. 1 tacet)

- don, sir. _ The gang - ster of love ___ rides a - gain. _____

Harmonica Solo

Gtr. 1: w/Rhy. Fig. 2, (4 times) w/Rhy. Fig. 6, (2 times)
N.C.

(I got the

Chorus

Gtr. 3: w/Rhy. Fig. 5

You know I got a chill. ___ It gim-me such a thrill. ___

fe - ver, _____ fe - ver, _____

Gtr. 1

let ring - - - -|

Rhy. Fig. 6

Gtr. 1

28

Like a burn-in' plague. _____ yeah, get out-ta my way. _____ Fe-

fe - ver, _____ fe - ver.) _____

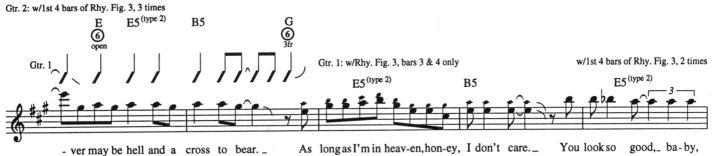

- ver may be hell and a cross to bear. _ As long as I'm in heav-en, hon-ey, I don't care. _ You look so good, _ ba-by,

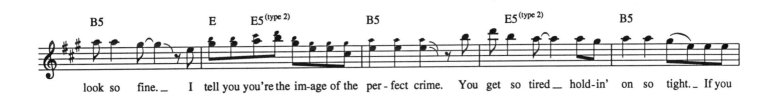

look so fine. _ I tell you you're the im-age of the per-fect crime. You get so tired _ hold-in' on so tight. _ If you

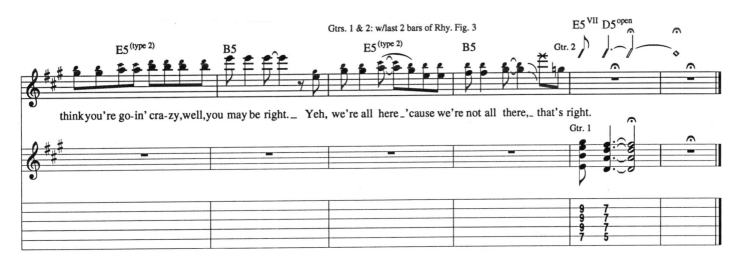

think you're go-in' cra-zy, well, you may be right. _ Yeh, we're all here _ 'cause we're not all there, _ that's right.

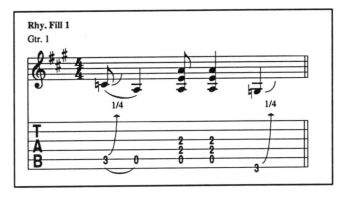

29

Livin' on the Edge

Words and Music by Steven Tyler, Joe Perry and Mark Hudson

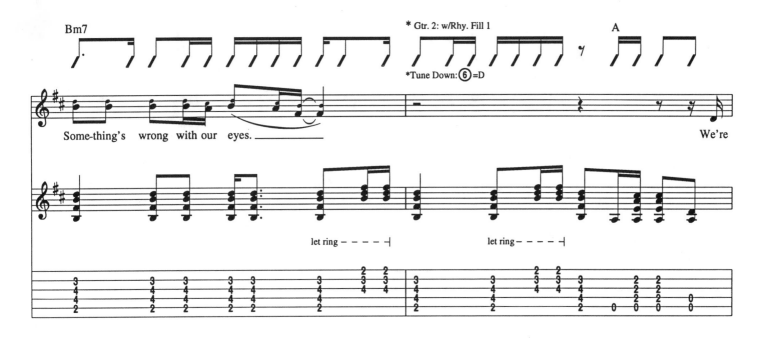

Some-thing's wrong with our eyes. _____ We're

see-ing things ___ in a diff-'rent way ___ and God knows it ain't his. ___ It

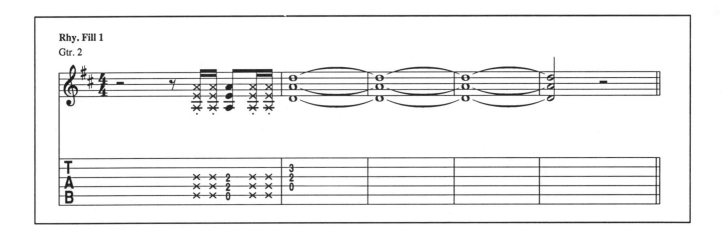

Rhy. Fill 1

Gtr. 2

Bm7

sure ain't no sur - prise. Yeah! We're liv - in' on the

let ring

let ring

***Chorus**
Gtr. 3: w/Riff B, (4 times)

D5
Rhy. Fig. 1

edge. Liv - in' on the

*Bass pedals D.

Riff A
Gtr. 1

End Riff A

ƒ let ring

sim.

full

full

Rhy. Fig. 1A
Gtr. 2

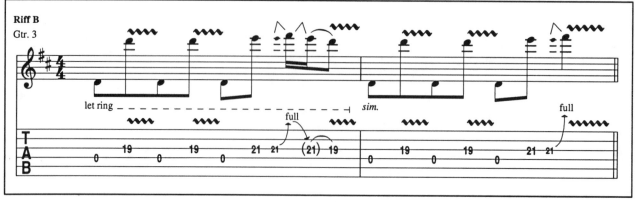

Riff B
Gtr. 3

let ring

sim.

full

full

Gtr. 1: w/Riff A, 3 times

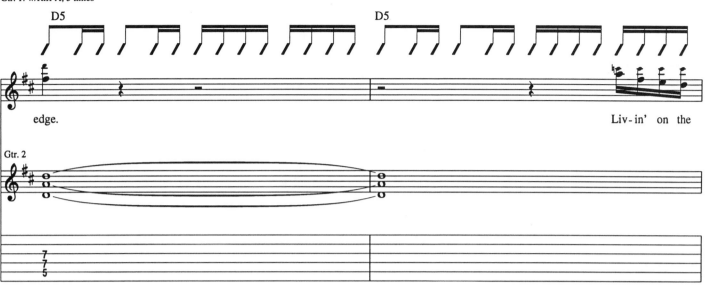

edge.

Liv-in' on the

Gtr. 2

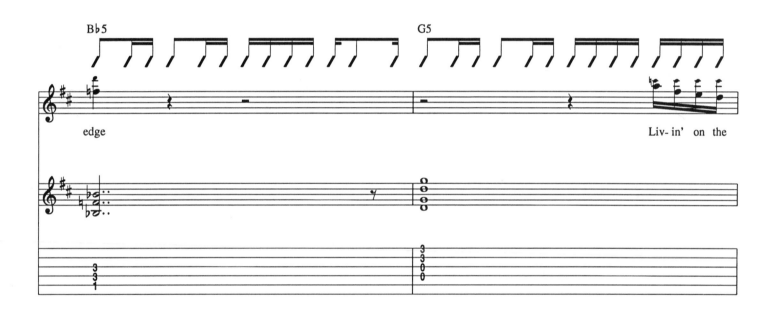

edge

Liv-in' on the

End Rhy. Fig. 1

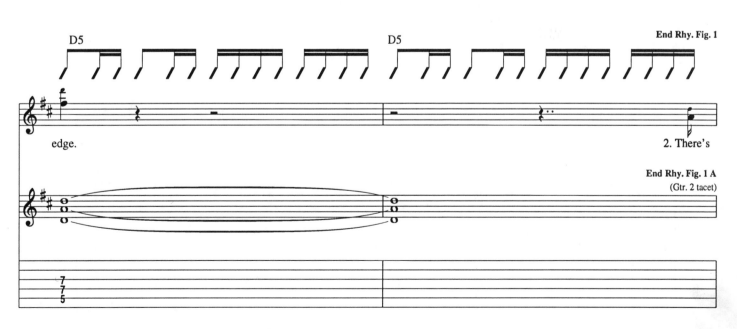

edge.

2. There's

End Rhy. Fig. 1 A
(Gtr. 2 tacet)

Verse

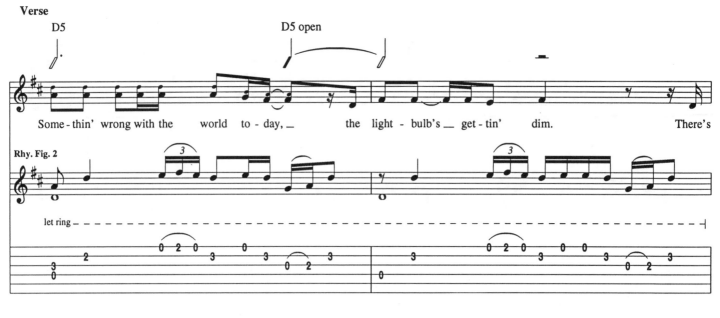

Some - thin' wrong with the world to - day, __ the light - bulb's __ get - tin' dim. There's

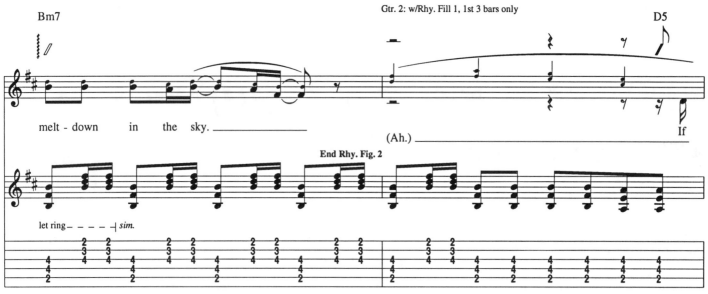

melt - down in the sky. _____ (Ah.) _____ If

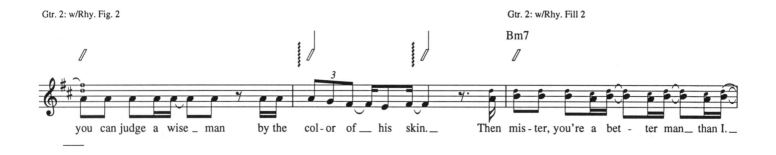

you can judge a wise __ man by the col - or of __ his skin. __ Then mis - ter, you're a bet - ter man __ than I. __

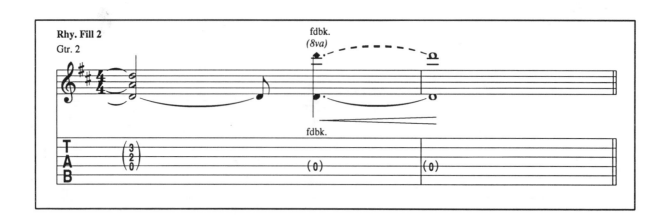

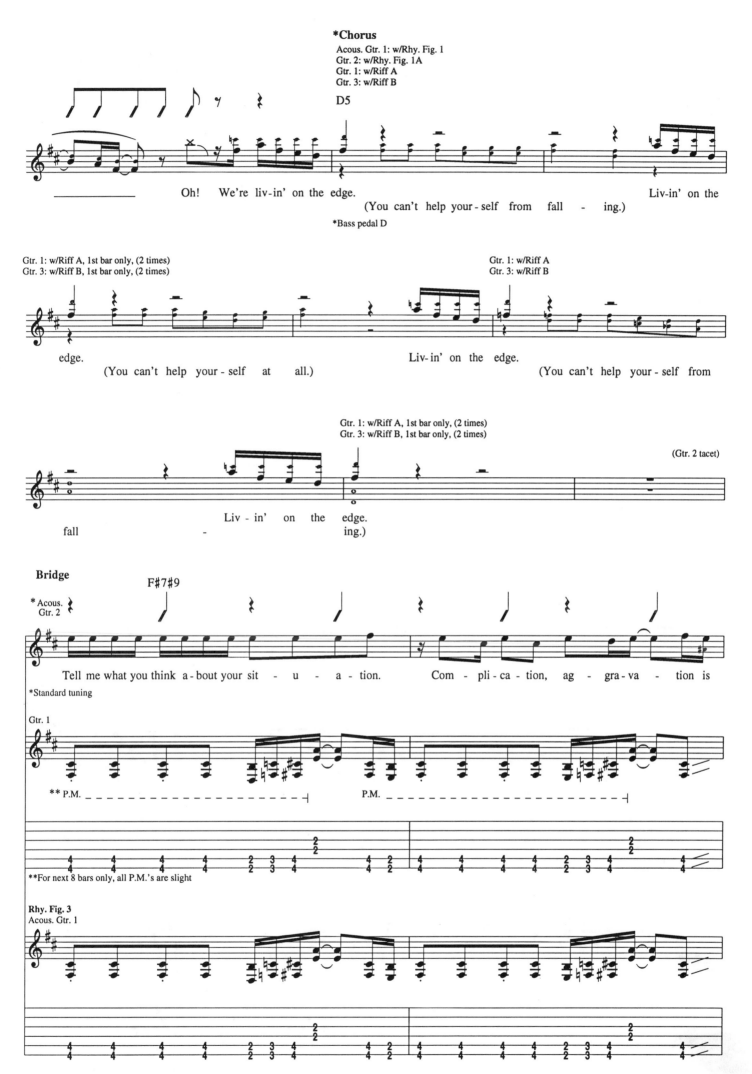

get - ting to you. _____ Yeah! If

(Acous. Gtr. 2 tacet)

Chick-en Lit - tle tells you that the sky is fall - in, ___ e - ven if it was-n't would you still come crawl - ing

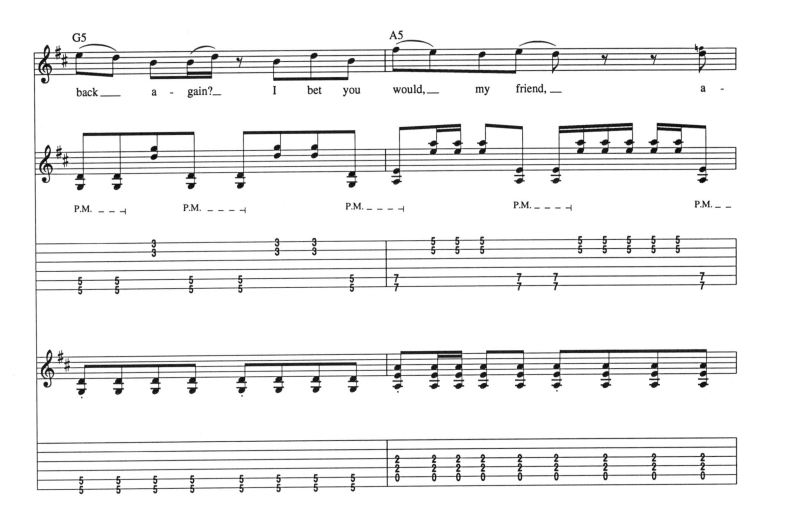

back ___ a - gain? ___ I bet you would, ___ my friend, ___ a -

gain and a - gain and a - gain and a - gain and a -

End Rhy. Fig. 3

Guitar Solo

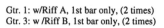

Gtr. 1: w/Riff A, 1st bar only, (2 times)
Gtr. 3: w /Riff B, 1st bar only, (2 times)

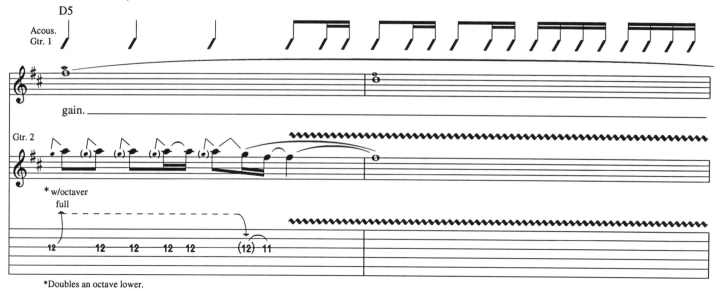

*Doubles an octave lower.

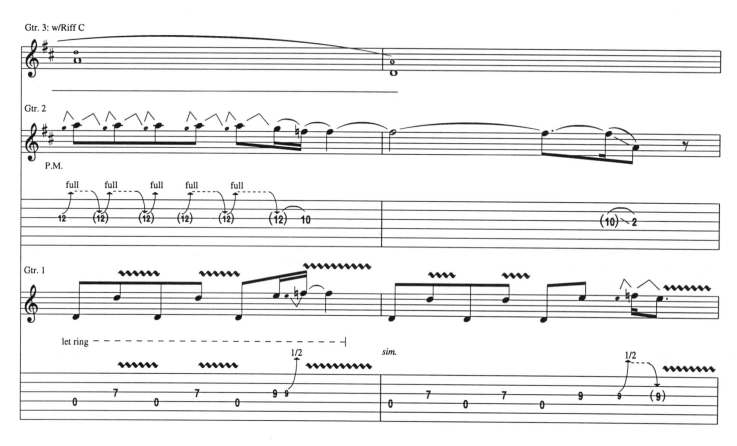

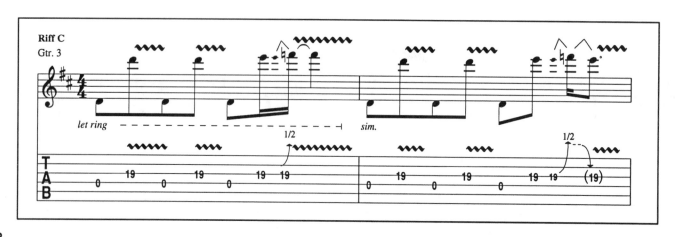

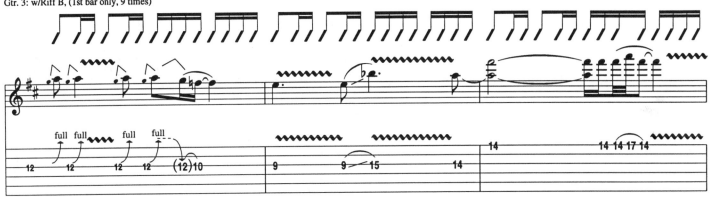

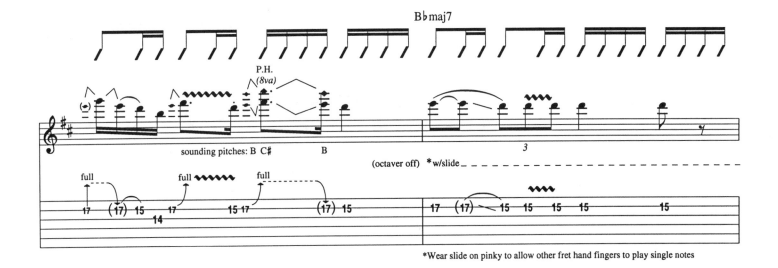

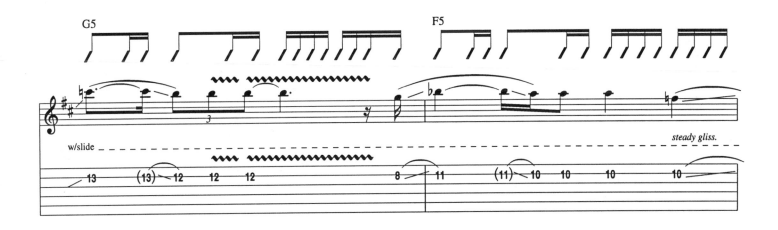

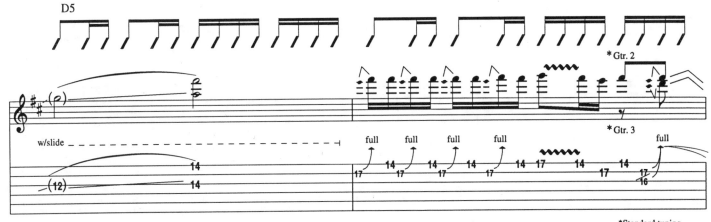

Bridge

Acous. Gtr. 1: w/Rhy. Fig. 3

F#7#9

Tell me what you think a-bout your sit - u - a - tion. Com - pli - ca - tion, ag - gra - va - tion is

(Gtrs. 2 & 3 tacet)

Gtr. 1

*P.M. — — — — — — — — — —   P.M. — — — — — — — — — —

*For next 9 bars only, all P.M.'s are slight.

get - ting to you. _____ Yeah! ____ If

P.M. — — — — —   full   1/2   1/2   1/2

Chick-en Lit - tle tells you that the sky is fall - in,__ e - ven if it was would you still come crawl - ing

(Acous. Gtr. 2 tacet)

P.M. — — — — — — —   P.M. — — — — — — —   P.M. — —

40

Verse

Gtr. 1: w/Riff A, (1st bar only, 9 times)
Gtr. 3: w/Riff B, (1st bar only, 9 times)
Gtr. 4: w/Riff D, till end

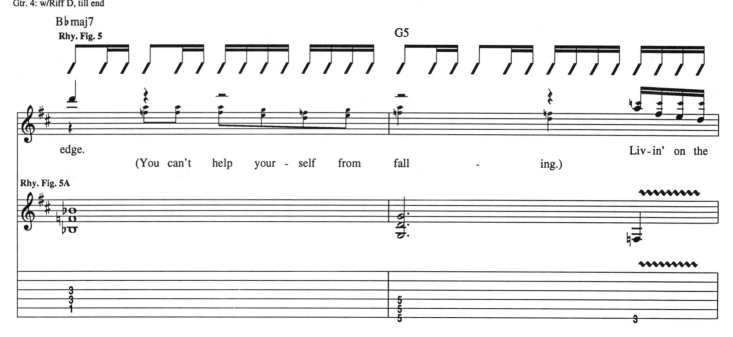

edge. (You can't help your-self from fall - ing.) Liv-in' on the

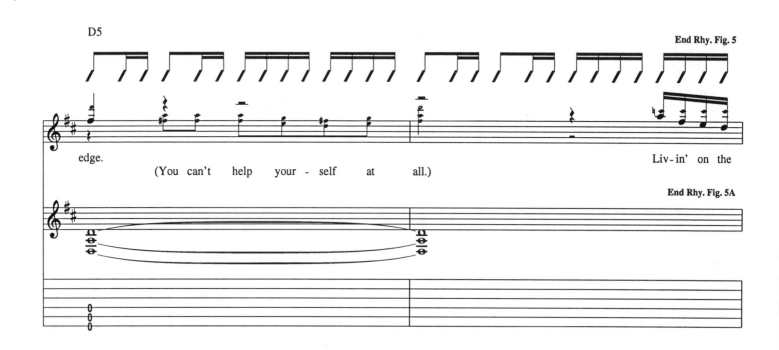

edge. (You can't help your-self at all.) Liv-in' on the

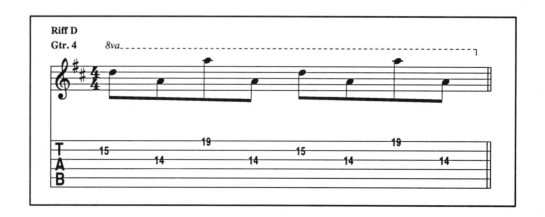

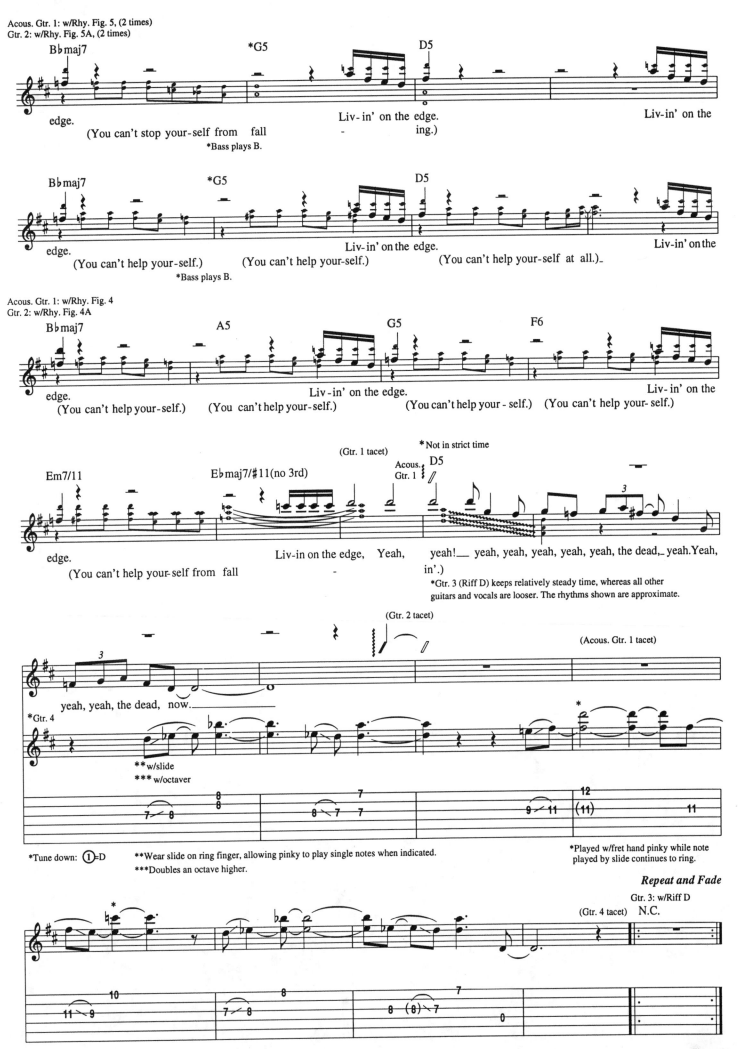

Flesh

Words and Music by Steven Tyler, Joe Perry and Desmond Child

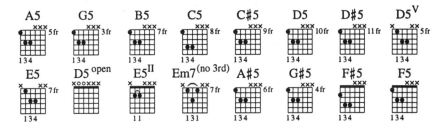

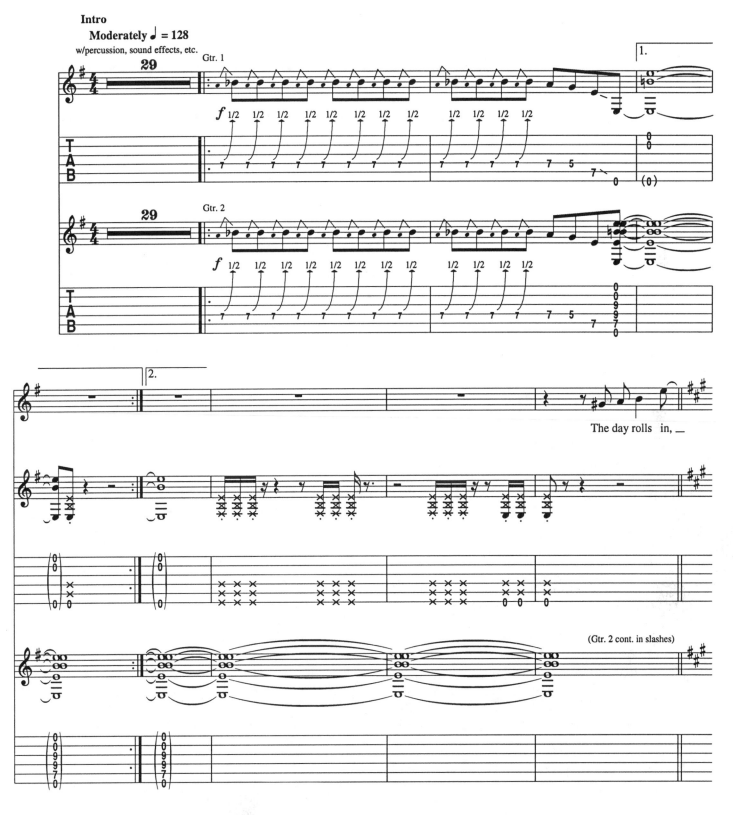

The day rolls in, —

(Gtr. 2 cont. in slashes)

Verse

Gtr. 1: w/Rhy. Fig. 1, 4 times

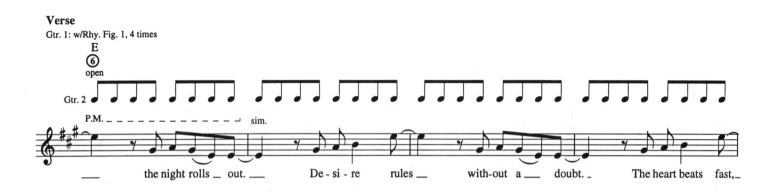

the night rolls __ out. __ De - si - re rules __ with-out a __ doubt. __ The heart beats fast,

__ you sal - i - vate. __ And when you come __ it won't be __ late. __ I guess by now

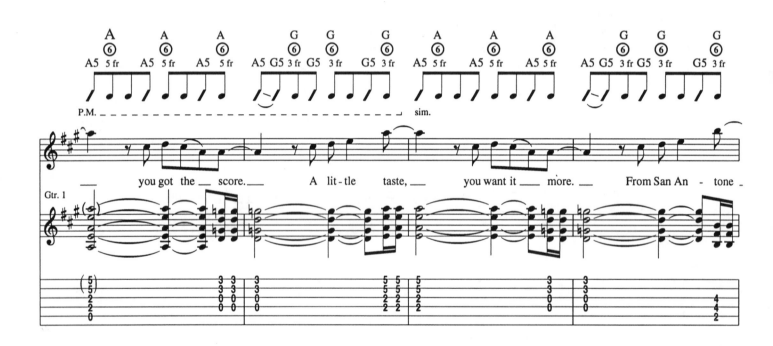

you got the __ score. __ A lit - tle taste, __ you want it __ more. __ From San An - tone

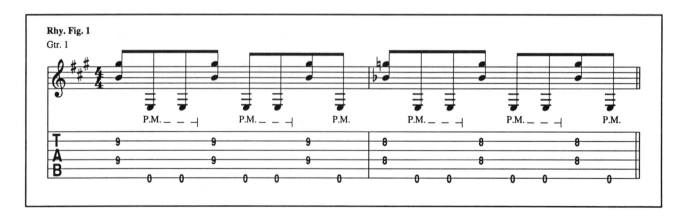

Rhy. Fig. 1

Gtr. 1

to Mar-ra-kesh, ___ yeah,__ when the night ___ comes __ ev - 'ry-bod-y got-ta have

Chorus

flesh! _____
(Flesh.) _____
You got me all soak - in' wet. __
Flesh!_

Gtr. 1: w/Rhy. Fig. 2A

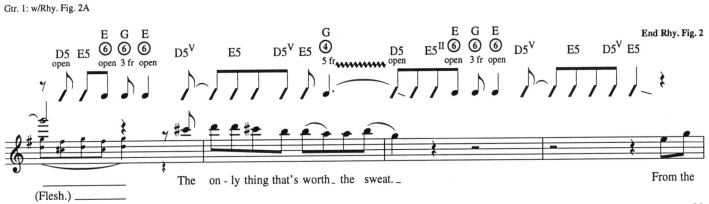

_____
(Flesh.) _____
The on - ly thing that's worth_ the sweat._
From the

2. The prince of lust _____ has met his ___ match. ___ The witch has brewed ___

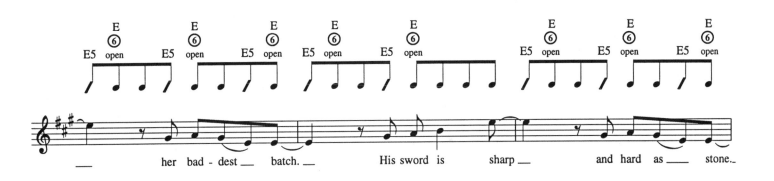

___ her bad - dest ___ batch. ___ His sword is sharp ___ and hard as ___ stone. ___

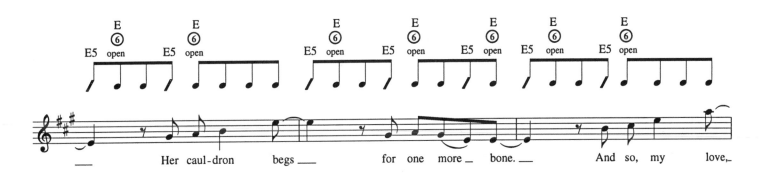

___ Her caul - dron begs ___ for one more ___ bone. ___ And so, my love, ___

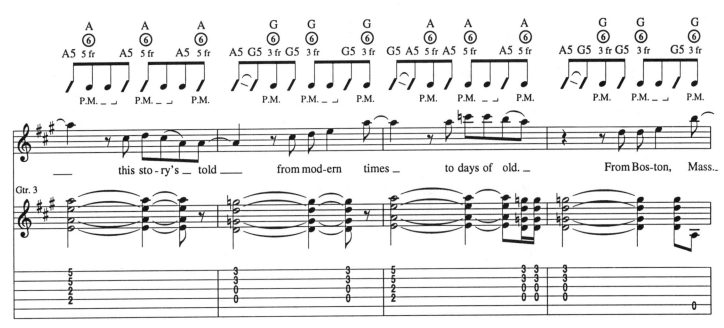

___ this sto - ry's ___ told ___ from mod - ern times ___ to days of old. ___ From Bos - ton, Mass. ___

Chorus

Gtr. 1: w/Rhy. Fig. 2A, (2 times)
Gtr. 2: w/Rhy. Fig. 2, (2 times)

Gtr. 2: w/Rhy. Fig. 3
Gtr. 3: w/Riff A

Gtr. 1

Gtr. 2: w/Fill 2

(Gtr. 1 cont. in slashes)

Fill 2
Gtr. 2

Interlude

Riff B

End Riff B

Riff C

End Riff C

Gtr. 2: w/Riff B
Gtr. 3: w/Riff C

Em7(no 3rd)

(Gtr. 1 cont. in notation)

Guitar Solo

*Low notes played w/pick, higher notes plucked w/middle finger (next 2 bars only.)
**Played behind the beat.

Rhy. Fig. 4

Walk On Down

Words and Music by Joe Perry

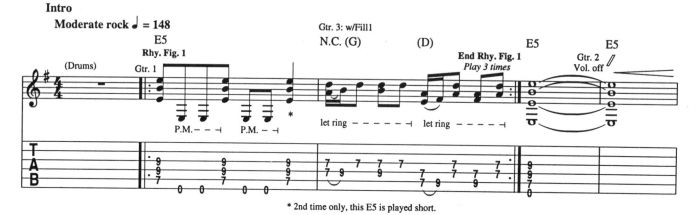

Intro

Moderate rock ♩ = 148

* 2nd time only, this E5 is played short.

𝄋 Verse

* Gtr. 1: w/Rhy. Fig. 1, (2 1/2 times)   Gtr. 3: w/Fill 1, (2 times)
  Gtr. 2: w/Rhy. Fig. 1, (3 times)

1. You won-der why_ you got holes in your shoes._ You won-der why_ they got more mon-ey than you._ You won-der why_ you got
2. See additional lyrics.

* Both gtrs. play slight variations of Rhy. Fig. 1 throughout the song.

Gtr. 3: w/Fill 1, (1st time), w/Fill 3, (2nd time)

noth-in' to lose. _ It makes no _ sense,_ don't try to fig-ure it out. _ You got-ta

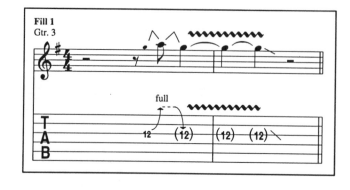

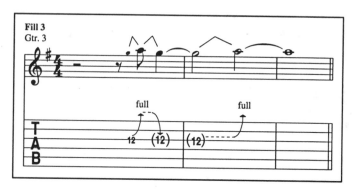

Chorus

walk on __ down. __   Walk on __ down. __

2nd time to Coda ⊕

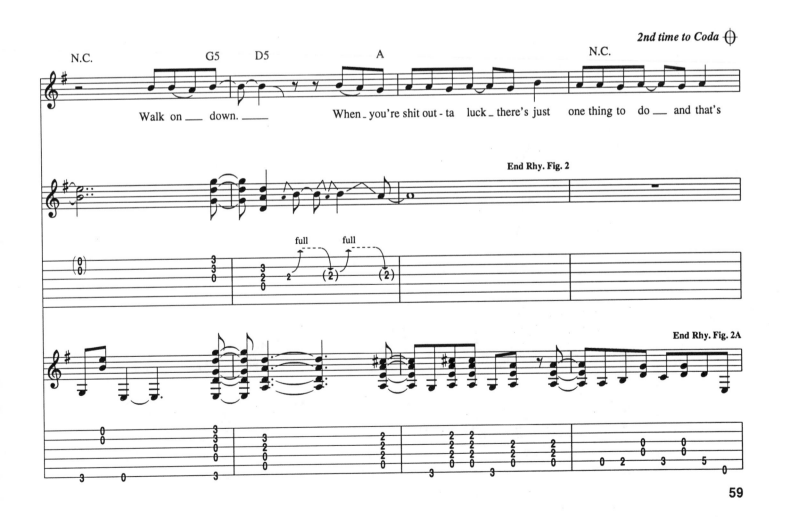

Walk on __ down. __   When __ you're shit out - ta luck __ there's just one thing to do __ and that's

⊕ *Coda*

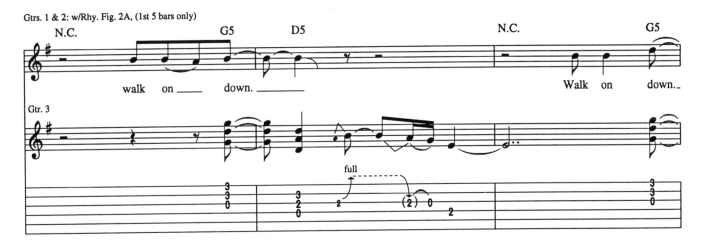

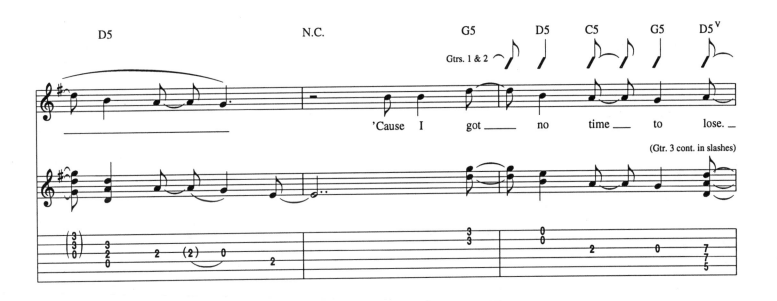

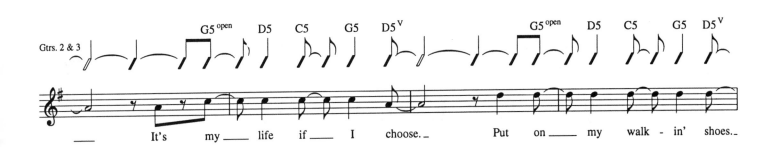

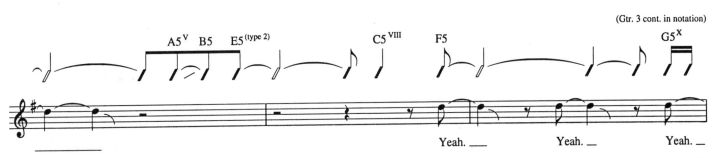

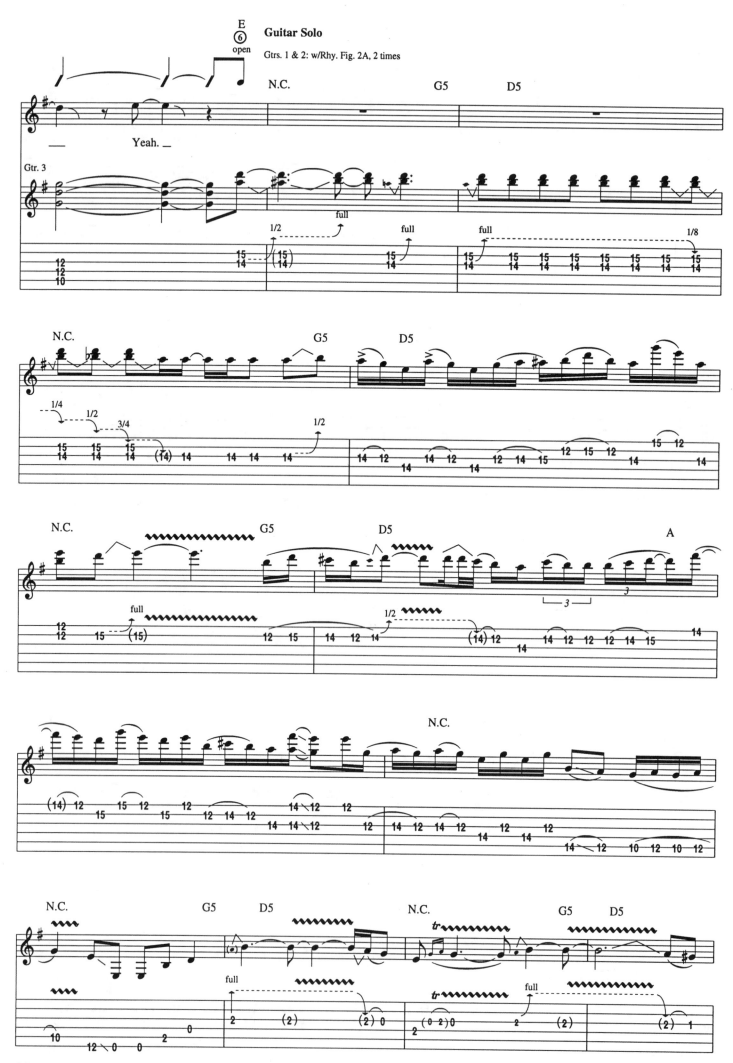

Chorus
Gtr. 4: w/Rhy. Fig. 2
Gtrs. 1 & 2: w/Rhy. Fig. 2A, (1st 6 bars only)

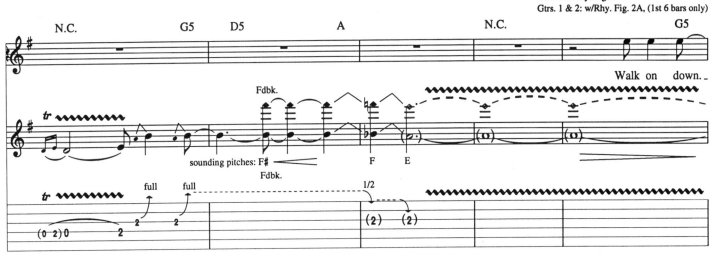

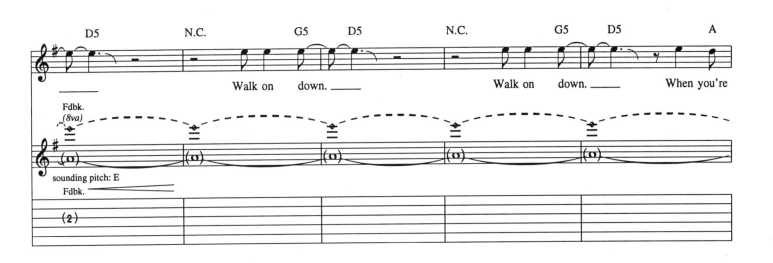

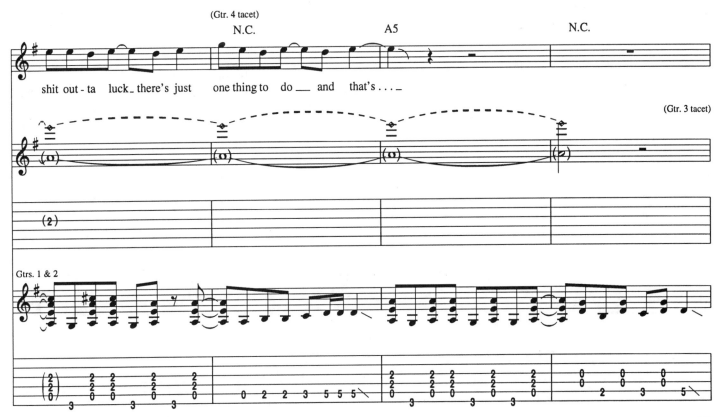

Guitar Solo

Gtrs. 1 & 2: w/Rhy. Fig. 2A, (3 times)

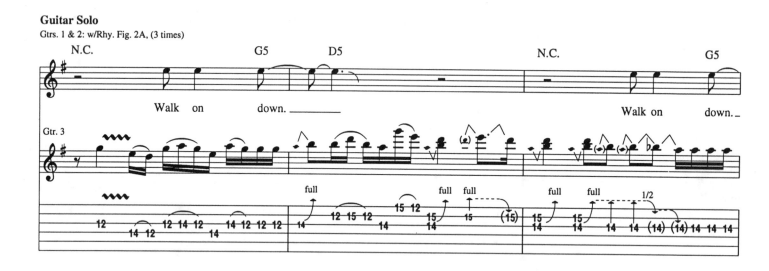

Walk on down. _____ Walk on down. _

Gtr. 3

Walk on down. _____ When you're

shit out-ta luck __ there's just one thing to do __ and that's _____ walk on down._

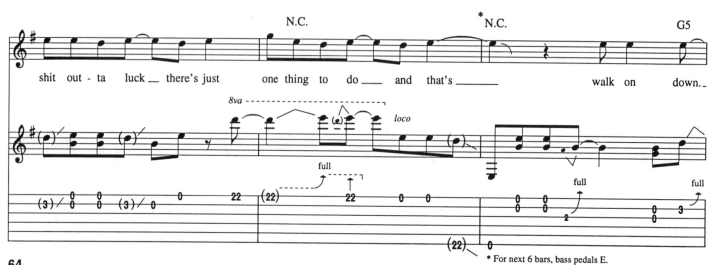

64

* For next 6 bars, bass pedals E.

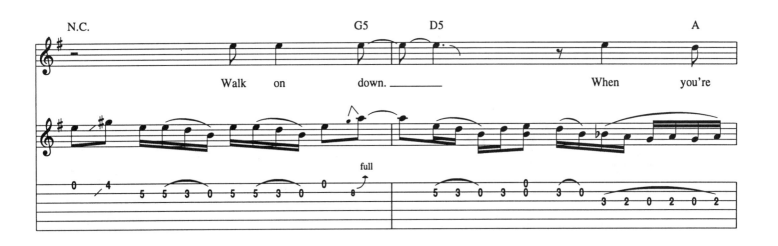

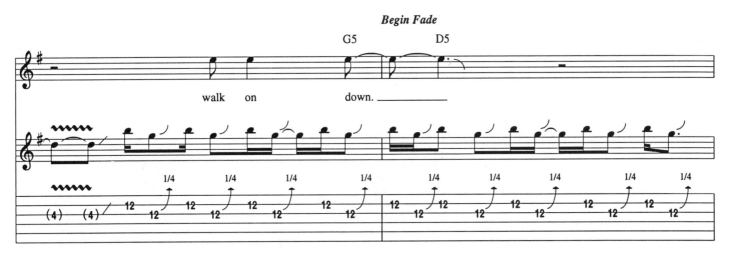

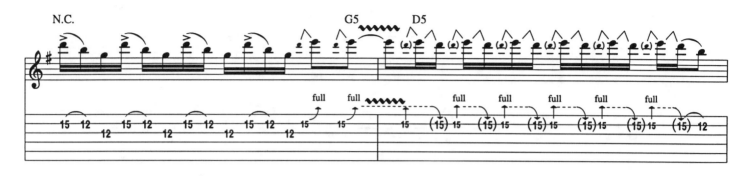

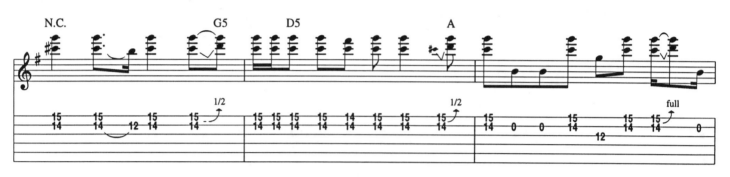

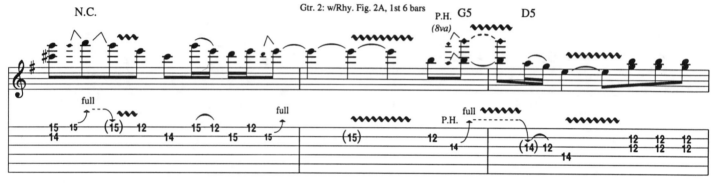

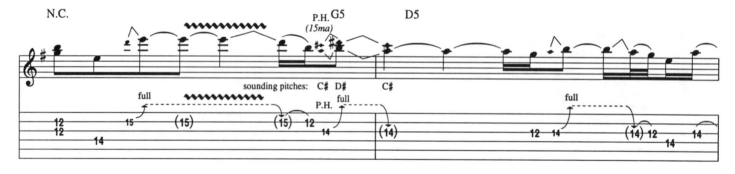

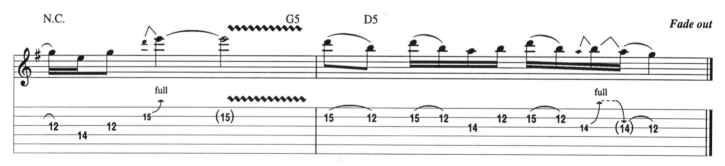

Additional Lyrics:

Well, she says that she loves ya,
In your mind there's no doubt.
But you feel like a stranger
When the lights go out.
As you lie there awake you think,
"This ain't no gift."
Don't try to figure,
That weight's too heavy to lift. *(To Chorus)*

Shut Up And Dance

Words and Music by Steven Tyler, Joe Perry, Jack Blades and Tommy Shaw

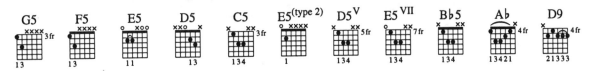

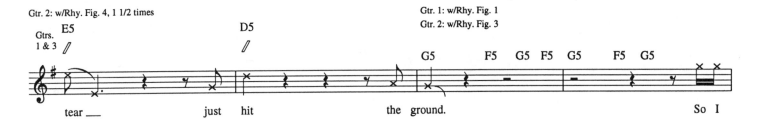

tear ___ just hit the ground. So I

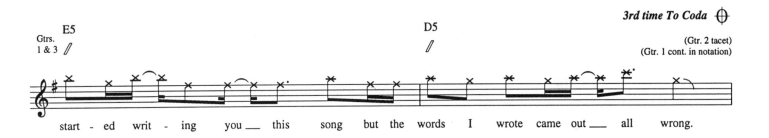

start - ed writ - ing you ___ this song but the words I wrote came out ___ all wrong.

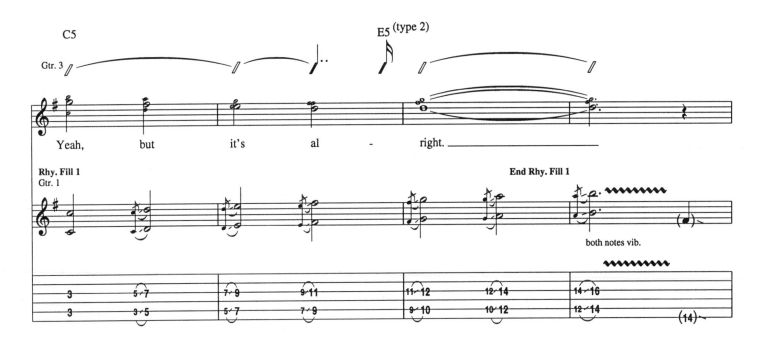

Yeah, but it's al - right. _____

Talk is cheap. Shut up and dance. ___ Ah! _____

Chorus

Gtr. 1: w/Rhy. Fig. 1, (4 times)
Gtr. 3: w/Rhy. Fig. 2, (3 times)

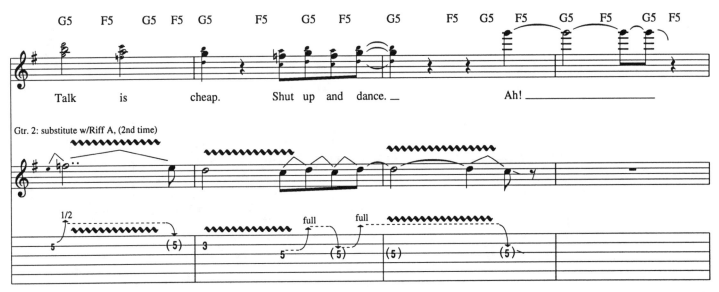

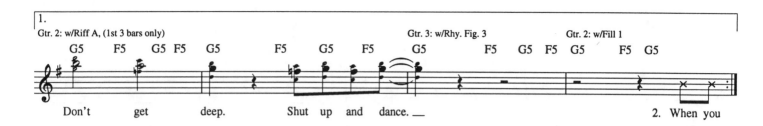

Gtr. 2: w/Riff A, (1st 3 bars only) Gtr. 3: w/Rhy. Fig. 3 Gtr. 2: w/Fill 1

Don't get deep. Shut up and dance. ___

2. When you

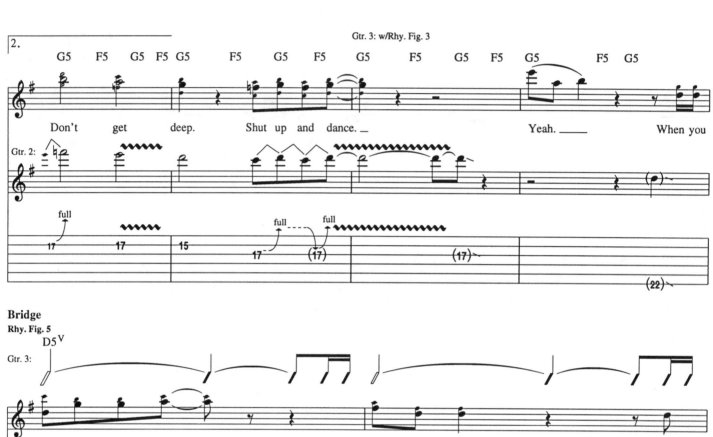

Don't get deep. Shut up and dance. ___ Yeah. ___ When you

Bridge
Rhy. Fig. 5

work your fin - gers ___ to the bone. Now

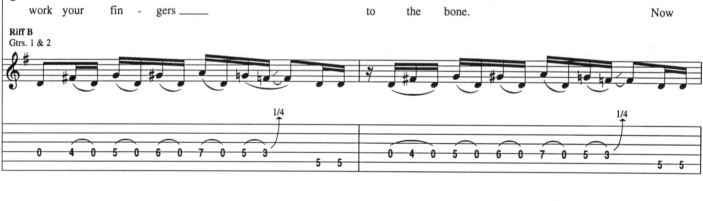

Riff B
Gtrs. 1 & 2

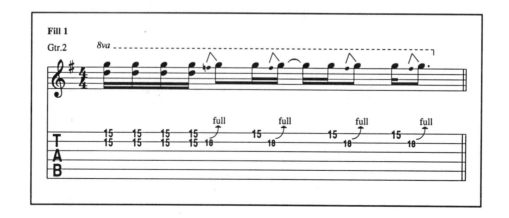

Fill 1
Gtr. 2

He wears the dress,   she wears the pants.   Here comes Jill and she needs ro-mance, but you can't do jack so shut up and dance!

Guitar Solo

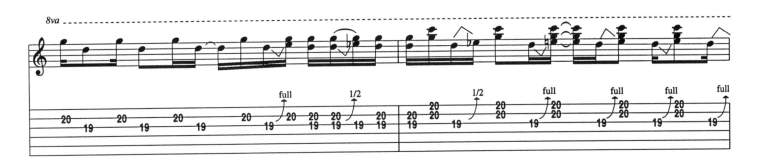

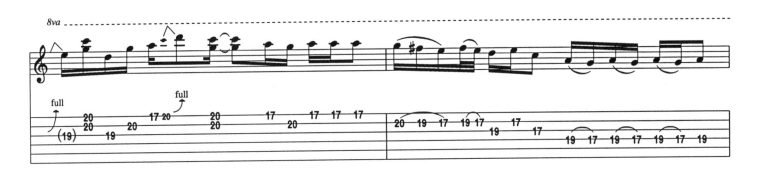

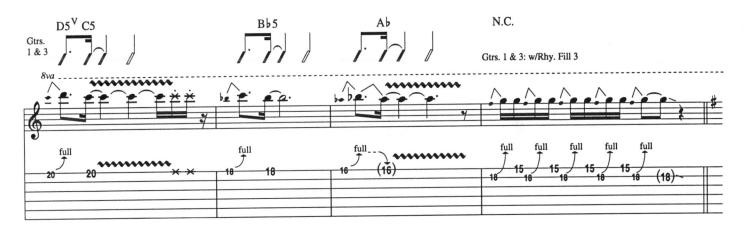

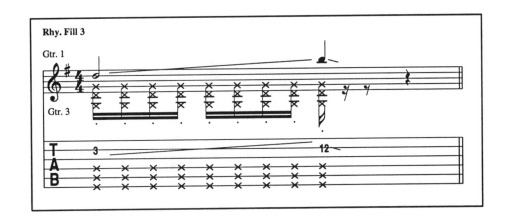

Gtr 1: w/Rhy. Fig. 1, (2 times)
Gtr 3: w/Rhy. Fig. 2

Gtr. 3: w/Rhy. Fig. 3

D.S. al Coda

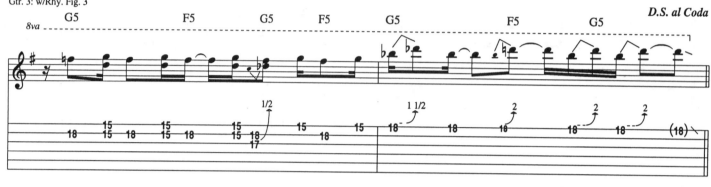

$\oplus$ *Coda*

Gtr. 1: w/Rhy. Fill 1

Gtr. 3: w/Rhy. Fill 6, (4 times)

Gtr. 1: w/Rhy. Fill 4

Gtr. 1: w/Rhy. Fill 6, (2 times)

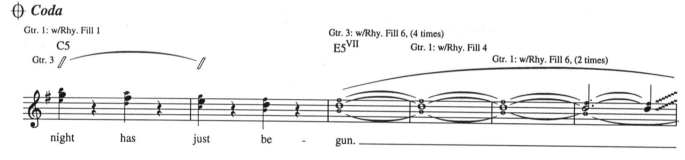

night   has   just   be - gun.

Gtr. 3: w/Rhy. Fig. 6A, (3 times)

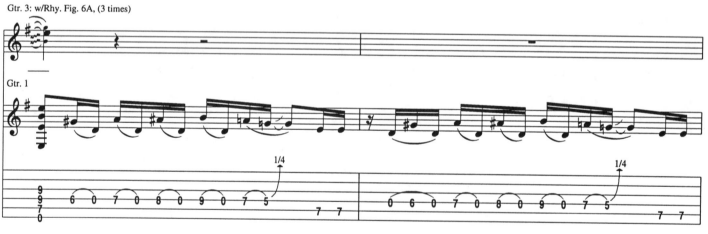

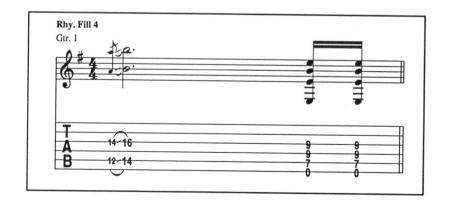

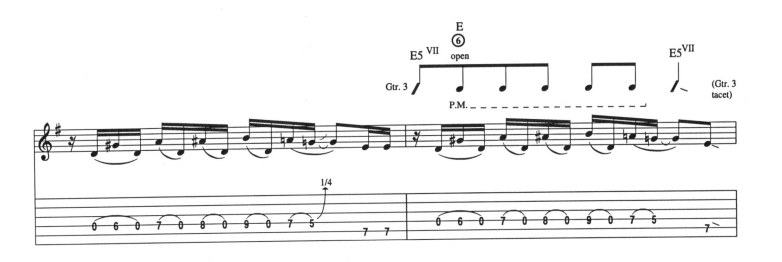

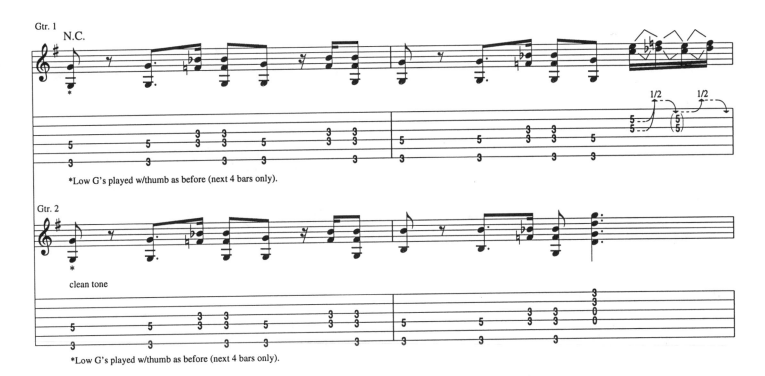

*Low G's played w/thumb as before (next 4 bars only).

*Low G's played w/thumb as before (next 4 bars only).

Additional Lyrics:

2. When you can't define the crime,
Then life ain't worth a dime.
When they take away everything you got
And they rub your nose in the funky spot.
Not without a fight. *(To Chorus)*

3. Sex is like a gun.
You aim, you shoot, you run.
When you're splittin' hairs with Mr. Clean,
It's like gettin' head from a guillotine.
And the night has just begun.

Cryin'

Words and Music by Steven Tyler, Joe Perry and Taylor Rhodes

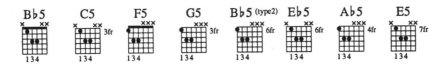

Intro

Moderately slow rock ♩. = 70

*Gtr. 2 w/semi-clean tone, Gtr. 3 w/distortion.

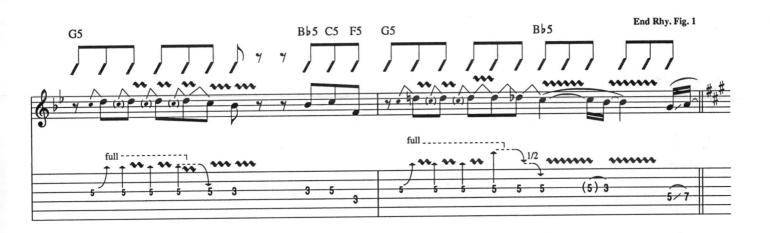

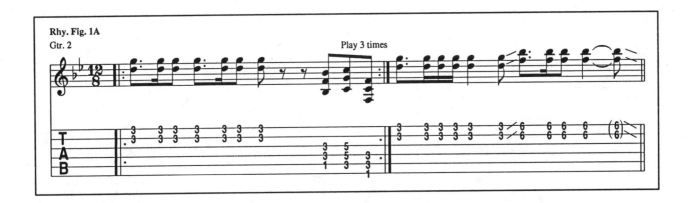

That kind of love ___ was the kill-in' kind. ___ Lis-ten!

(Gtr. 4 tacet)

Pre-chorus

All I want ___ is some-one I can't re-sist.

Rhy. Fig. 2

Gtr. 3

I know all I need to know by the way that I got kissed. ___ I was

End Rhy. Fig. 2

do what you do _____ down on me. _____ Yeah!

End Rhy. Fig. 3

*Gtr. 1 to left of slash in TAB.

Gtr. 3: w/Rhy. Fig. 1
Gtr. 2: w/Rhy. Fig. 1A

Now there's not e-ven breath-in' room _____ be-tween plea-sure and pain.

Yeah, you cry when we're mak-in' love. _____ Must be one and the same. _____

(Gtr. 1 tacet)

Verse

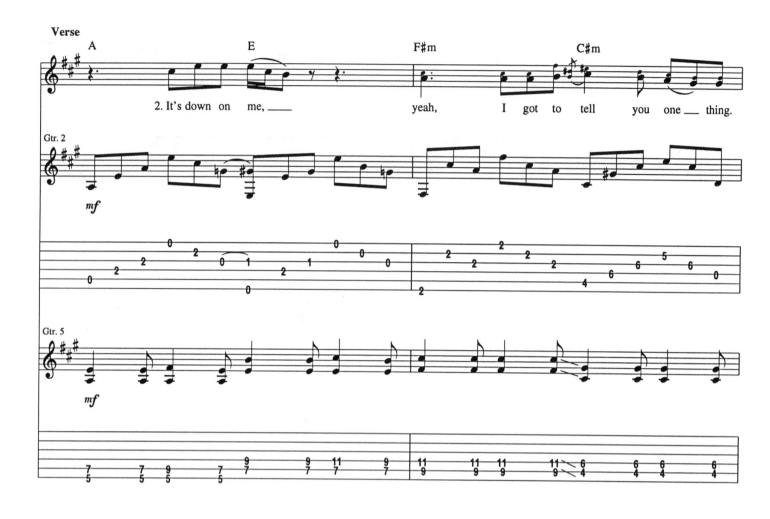

2. It's down on me, _____ yeah, I got to tell you one _____ thing.

Gtr. 2

Gtr. 5

It's been on my mind, _____ girl, I got-ta say. _____

Guitar Solo

Gtr. 3: w/Rhy. Fig. 1, (1st 3 bars only)
Gtr. 2: w/Rhy. Fig. 1A, (1st 3 bars only)

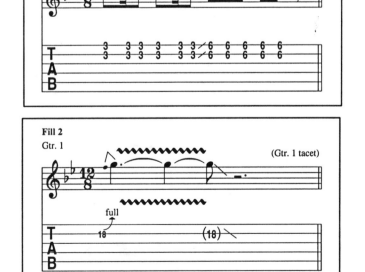

-y. _____ I was cry - in' just to get you. Now I'm dy - in' to let you ___

do what you, do what you do down to me, ba-by, ba-by, ba-by, ba-by, ba-by, ba-by.

Harmonica Solo

Gtr. 2: w/Rhy. Fig. 4, (simile)

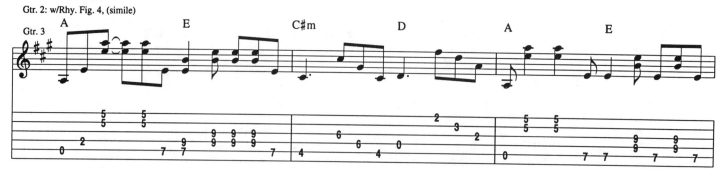

Gtr. 2: w/Rhy. Fill 2

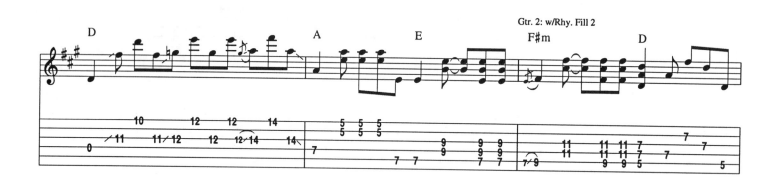

Gtr. 2: w/Rhy. Fig. 4A, (simile)

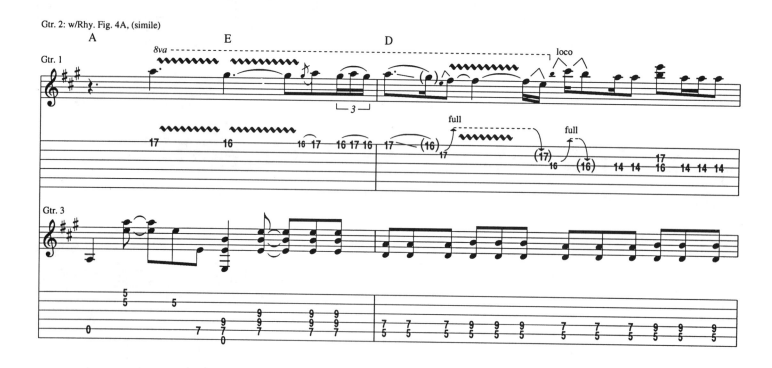

Rhy. Fill 2
Gtr. 2

Outro

Gtr. 2: w/Rhy. Fig. 4, (simile)

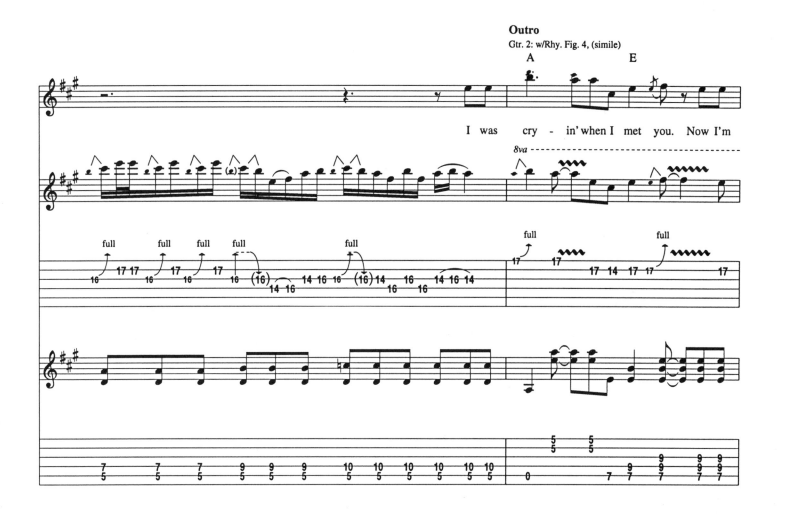

I was cry - in' when I met you. Now I'm

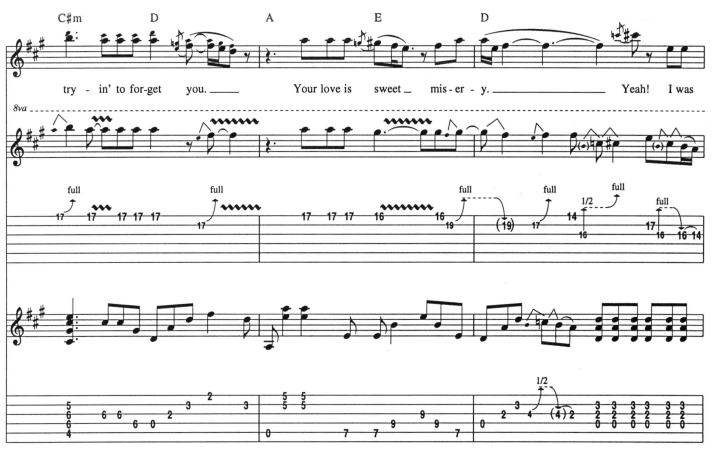

try - in' to for-get you. _____ Your love is sweet _ mis-er - y. _____ Yeah! I was

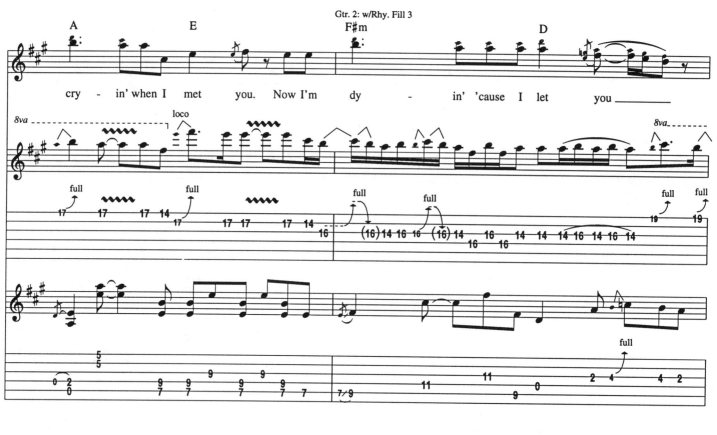

cry - in' when I met you. Now I'm dy - in' 'cause I let you _____

do ____ what you do _____ down to, down to, down to, down to, down to.

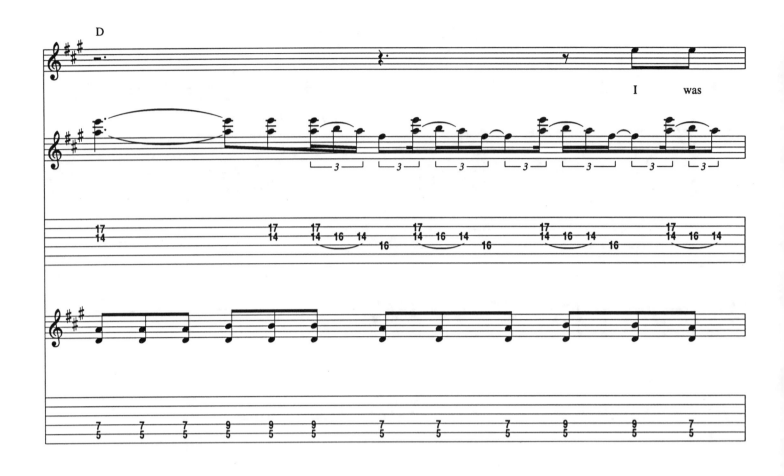

I was

Fade

cry - in' ___ when I met you. Now I'm dy - in' ___ 'cause I let you. ___

Gotta Love It

Words and Music by Steven Tyler, Joe Perry and Mark Hudson

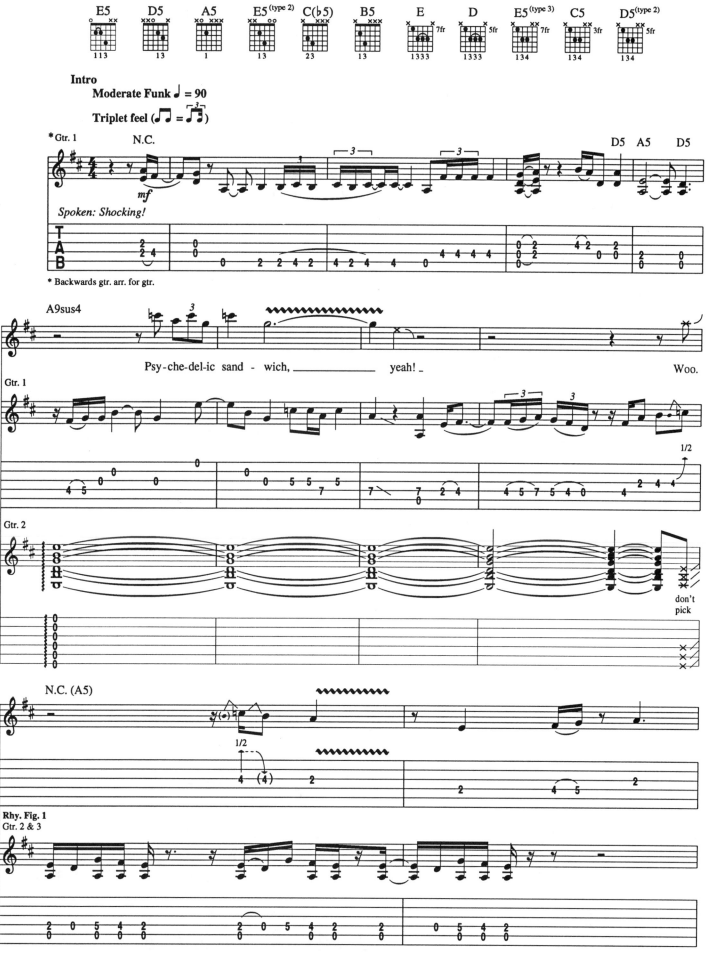

Rhy. Fig. 2A

E5

Gtr. 2

End Rhy. Fig. 2A

Rhy. Fig. 2
Gtr. 3

End Rhy. Fig. 2

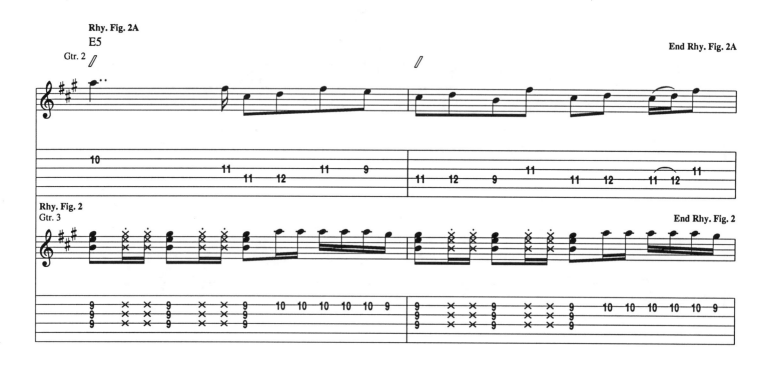

Verse
w/backwards gtr. ad lib (next 8 bars)

Rhy. Fig. 3A

1. An - y way you can feel it. ___ You should-n't try to con - ceal it, ba - by.

Rhy. Fig. 3

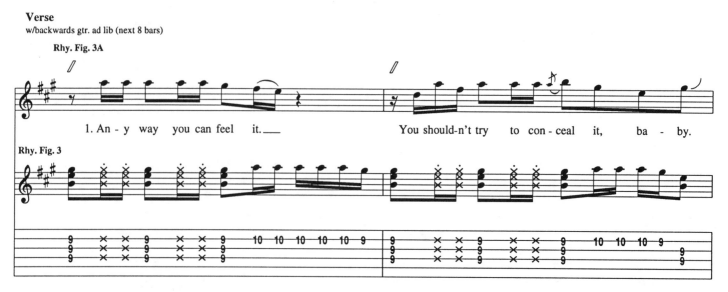

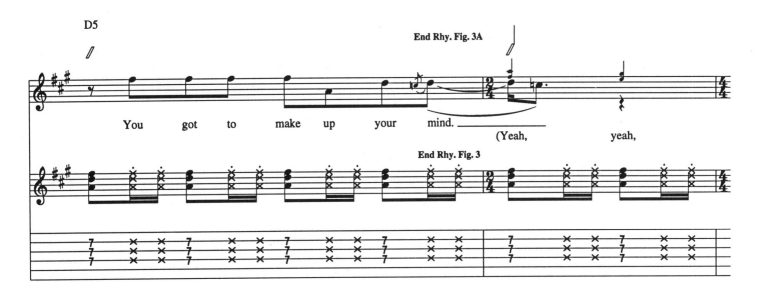

D5

You got to make up your mind. _____ (Yeah, yeah,

End Rhy. Fig. 3A

End Rhy. Fig. 3

E5

Rhy. Fig. 4A

An-y way I can steal it. _____ An-y way you can deal it to me.

yeah.)

Rhy. Fig. 4

D5

A-you know the plea-sure's all mine. _____ (Yeah, yeah, yeah.) _____

End Rhy. Fig. 4A

End Rhy. Fig. 4

Chorus

Gtrs. 2 & 3: w/Rhy. Fig 1, (2 times)

N.C. (A5)

You got-ta love it. You bet-ter own it. _____ You got-ta love it. And God

knows it.   You got - ta shu - uh   shove it.   I'm gon - na make things hap - pen.

Go - in' round, _ 'n round, _ 'n round, _ 'n round, _ 'n round, _ 'n round, _ 'n round,_

Gtr. 1: w/Fill 2   Gtr. 3: w/Rhy. Fig. 2
                                                       Gtr. 2: w/Rhy. Fig. 2A

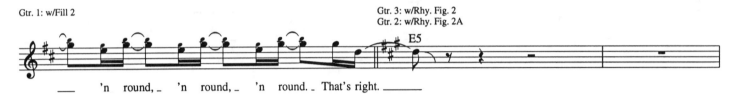

_ 'n round, _ 'n round, _ 'n round. _ That's right. _____

Verse

Gtr. 3: w/Rhy. Fig. 3
Gtr. 2: w/Rhy. Fig. 3A
w/backwards gtr. ad lib (next 9 bars)

2. I wan - na say you're a fire - crack - er.   I wan - na say you're a switch - blade knife.

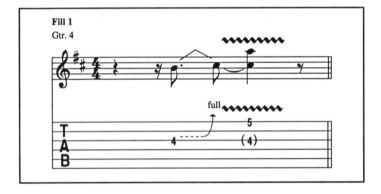

Fill 1
Gtr. 4

Fill 2
Gtr. 1

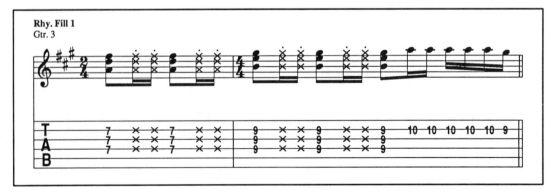

Rhy. Fill 1
Gtr. 3

You make your sex a ca - reer. _____

(Yeah, yeah, ___ yeah, yeah.) _

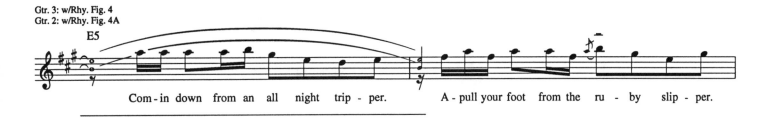

Gtr. 3: w/Rhy. Fig. 4
Gtr. 2: w/Rhy. Fig. 4A

Com - in down from an all night trip - per.

A - pull your foot from the ru - by slip - per.

Chorus
Gtr. 2 & 3: w/Rhy. Fig. 1, (2 times)

'Cause you can't get there from here. _____

(Yeah, yeah, yeah.) _____

You got - ta love it.

You bet - ter own it. _____

You got - ta love it.

And God

Gtr. 4: w/Fill 3

knows it.

You got - ta shu - uh shove it.

I'm gon - na make things hap - pen.

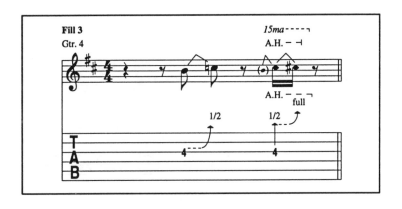

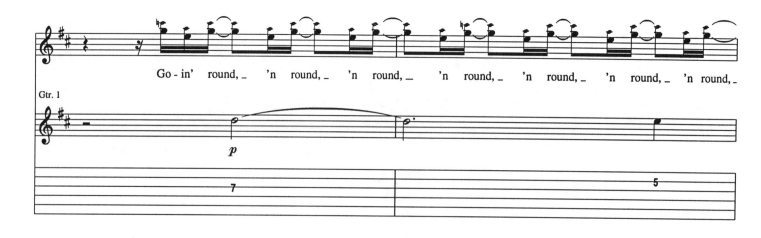

Go - in' round, __ 'n round, __ 'n round, __ 'n round, __ 'n round, __ 'n round, __ 'n round, __

Gtr. 1

p

7   5

Gtr. 3: w/Rhy. Fill 2

A5

Gtr. 2

__ 'n round, __ 'n round, __ 'n round, __ 'n round, __ 'n round, __ 'n round, __ 'n round, __ 'n round, __

5   7   7 2   4   2   4   2

__ 'n round, 'n round, __ 'n round, 'n round, __ 'n round, 'n round, 'n round, 'n round, __ 'n round, 'n round, 'n round. __

mf

(2)   4 0 2   5   4   4 5   5 5 0 5 7   7

Rhy. Fill 2
Gtr. 3

(Gtr. 3 tacet)

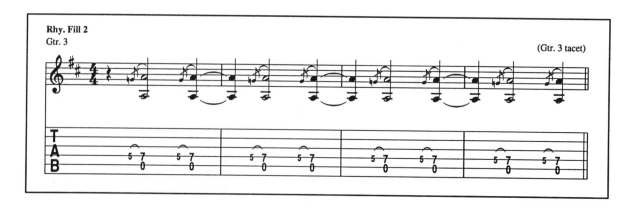

Gtr. 2: w/Riff A

N.C. (Em)

(Aah,   aah,   aah,   aah.)

full

Bridge
w/backwards gtr. ad lib (next 8 bars)

E5 (type 2)

Gtr. 3

I got this feel-ing deep in - side my _ gut.   O- ver-whelm-ing feel-ing of I know not   what. _

B5 B5 B5 B5   B5 B5 B5 B5
C(♭5) C(♭5) C(♭5) C(♭5)   C(♭5) C(♭5) C(♭5) C(♭5)
Gtrs.
2 & 3

One thing's for sure, I ain't got time for those who can't re - late. _____

Bass solo

End Rhy. Fig. 5

Rhy. Fig. 5   C   B   A   G
E   D   ⑤   ⑤   ⑤   ⑥
                                                                                   3 fr. 2 fr. open 3 fr.

Harm. _____

Gtr. 1

Harm. ___

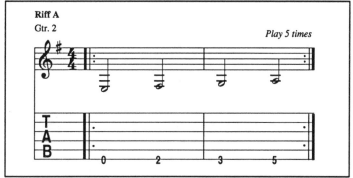

Riff A
Gtr. 2

Play 5 times

Guitar solo

Gtrs. 2 & 3: w/Rhy. Fig. 5

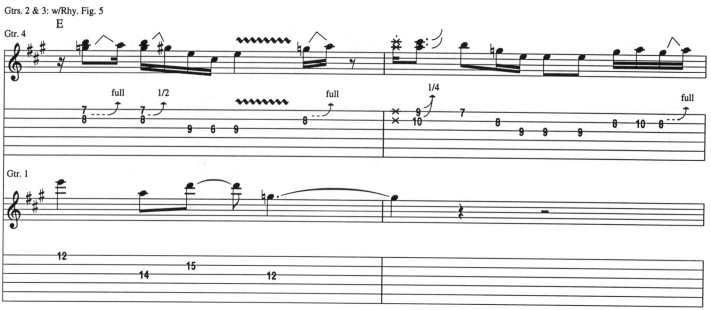

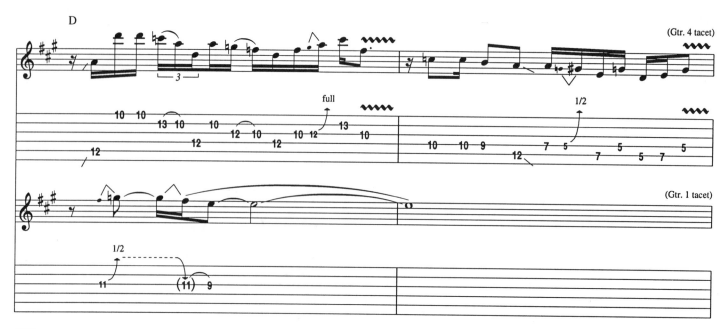

3. You got-ta learn to love the mid-night mad-ness.

You got-ta rev-el in the good and bad-ness, if yin 'n yang is your thing.

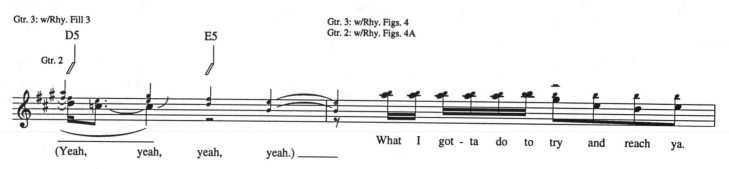

Gtr. 3: w/Rhy. Fill 3

Gtr. 3: w/Rhy. Figs. 4
Gtr. 2: w/Rhy. Figs. 4A

(Yeah, yeah, yeah, yeah.) What I got-ta do to try and reach ya.

Is it for real or just a dou-ble fea-ture. So let's go throw the I Ching.
(Yeah, yeah, yeah.)

Chorus

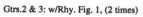

Gtrs.2 & 3: w/Rhy. Fig. 1, (2 times)

N.C. (A5)

You got-ta love it. You wan-na own it. You got-ta love it. And God

Gtr. 4: w/Fill 5

knows it. You got-ta shu-uh shove it. You got-ta make things hap-pen. Go-in' round,. 'n round, 'n round,.

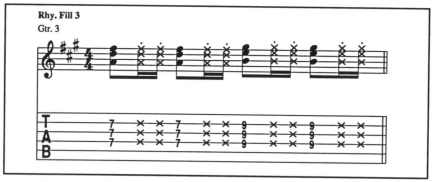

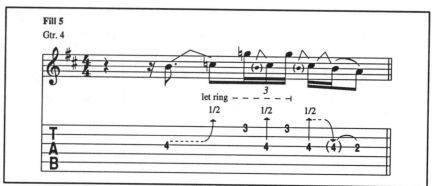

'n round, _ 'n round, _ 'n round, _ 'n round, _ 'n round, _ 'n round, _ 'n round, _ 'n round, _

Outro
Riff B

End Riff B

Gtr. 3

Gtr. 3: w/Riff B, (till end)

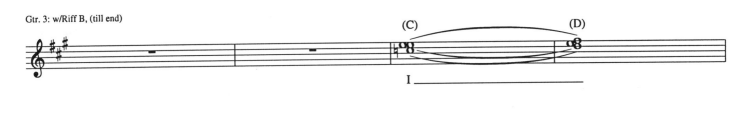

Crazy

Words and Music by Steven Tyler, Joe Perry and Desmond Child

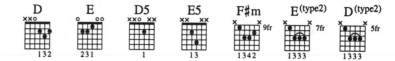

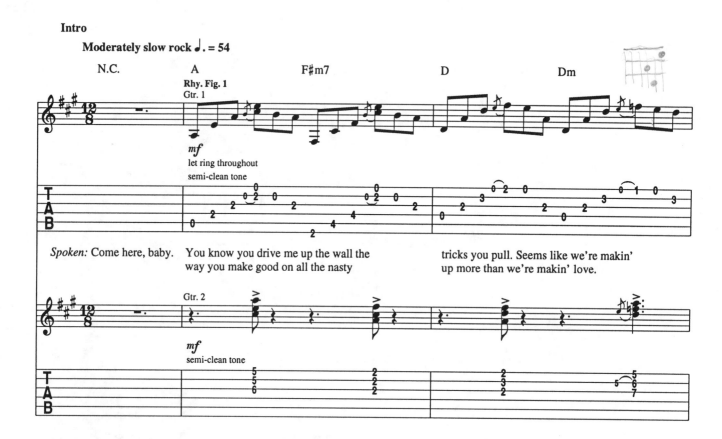

Spoken: Come here, baby. You know you drive me up the wall the way you make good on all the nasty tricks you pull. Seems like we're makin' up more than we're makin' love.

And it always seems you got somn' on your mind other than me. Girl, you got to change your crazy ways. You hear me?

Verse

1. Say you're leav-in' on a sev-en thir-ty train, and that you're head-in' out to Hol – ly - wood.

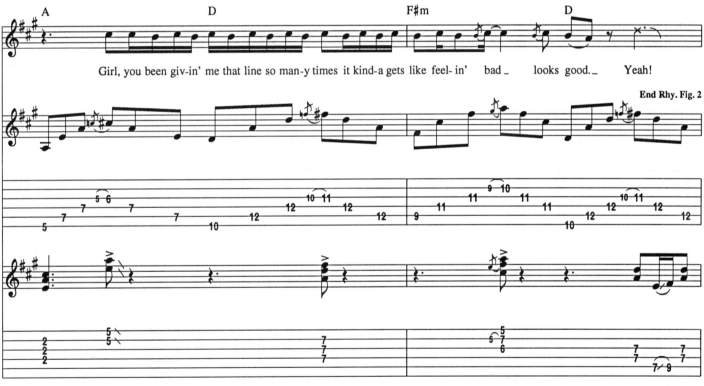

Girl, you been giv-in' me that line so man-y times it kind-a gets like feel-in' bad _ looks good. _ Yeah!

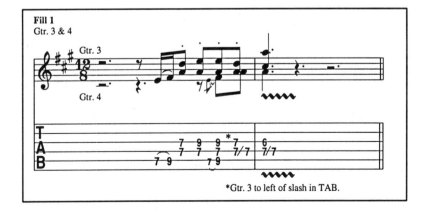

*Gtr. 3 to left of slash in TAB.

Gtr. 3: w/Fill 2

That kind-a lov-in'   turns a man __   to a slave. __

That kind-a lov-in'   sends a man __   right to his grave.   I go

Chorus

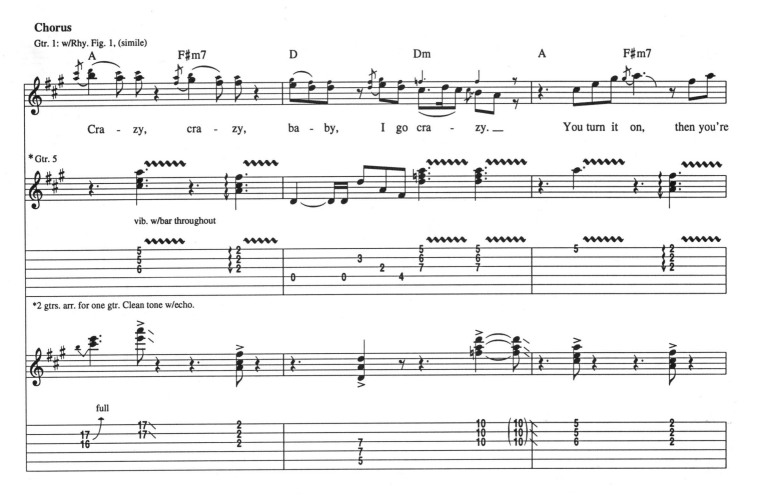

Cra - zy, cra - zy, ba - by, I go cra - zy. __ You turn it on, then you're

gone. __ Yeah, you drive __ me cra - zy, cra - zy, cra - zy for you ba - by. __

But, I know you ain't wear-in' noth-in' un-der-neath that o-ver-coat. ___ And it's all a show. ___ Yeah!

Pre-chorus

That kind - a lov - in' makes me wan-na pull ___ down the shade. ___ Yeah!

That_ kind-a lov-in', yeah, now I'm nev-er, nev-er, nev-er,_ nev-er gon-na be the same. I go

(Gtr. 6 tacet)

Chorus

Gtr. 1: w/Rhy. Fig. 1, (simile)

cra - zy, cra - zy, ba - by, I go cra - zy._ You turn it on, then you're

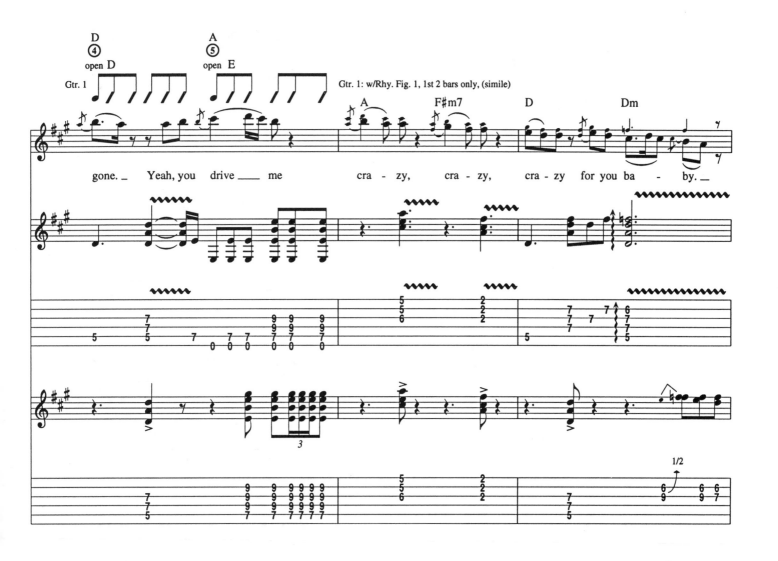

gone. _ Yeah, you drive ___ me cra - zy, cra - zy, cra - zy for you ba - by. _

What can I do, ___ hon - ey? I feel like the col - or ___ blue. ___

Guitar Solo

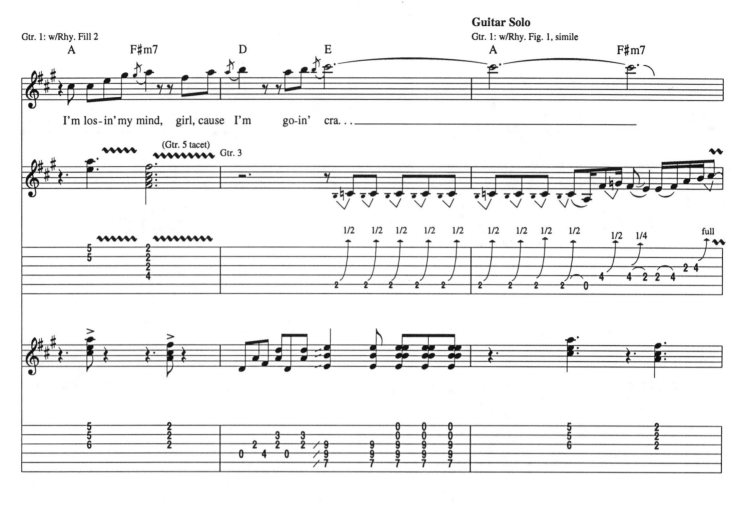

I'm los-in' my mind, girl, cause I'm go-in' cra...

Gtr. 1: w/Rhy. Fig. 1, (simile)

Gtr. 1: w/Rhy. Fill 3

Bridge

I need _____ your love.

Hon-ey, _____

Rhy. Fill 3
Gtr. 1

Gtr. 3: w/Fill 4
w/vocal ad libs (till end)

Gtr. 1: w/Rhy. Fig. 1, (simile)

Fade

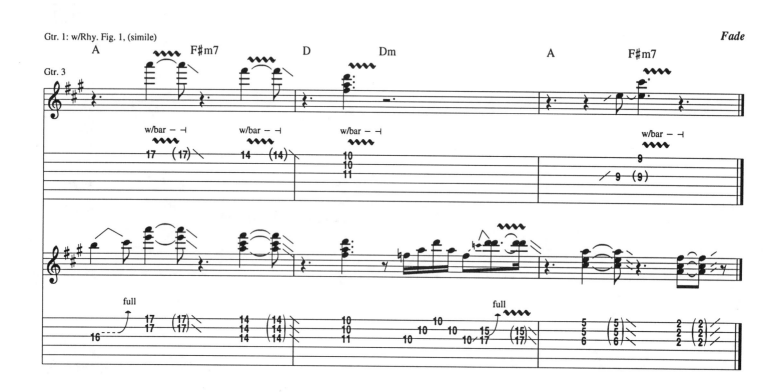

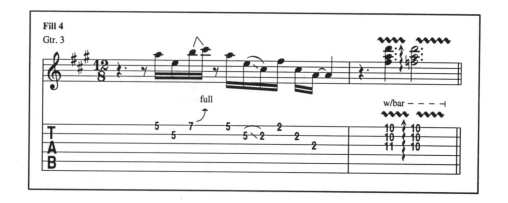

Line Up

Words and Music by Steven Tyler, Joe Perry and Lenny Kravitz

- ing gets tough,__ and your talk ___ ain't e - nough,. line up. (Line up.)
___ on a limb,_ and you wan - na come in, then line up. (Line up.)
___ wan - na live, _ then we all ___ got - ta give, _ line up. (line up.)

1, 3. We got - ta
2. Your

get up, get out be - fore__ they get us down. 'Cause liv - in' up a-gainst the wall,_ yeah, has got us locked
heads down, sit-tin' 'round. Pick yo face up off the ground and get yo - self to - geth- er, ba - by, and learn to stand

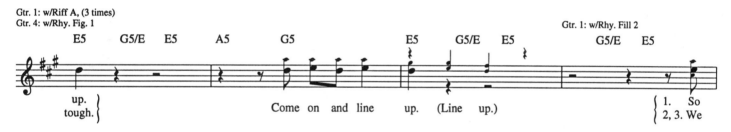

up. }
tough. }

Come on and line up. (Line up.)

1. So
2, 3. We

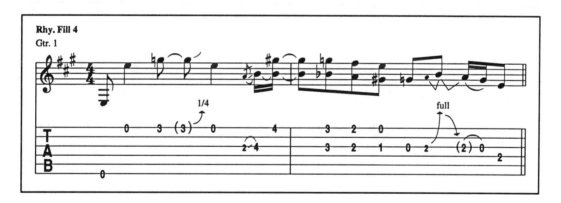

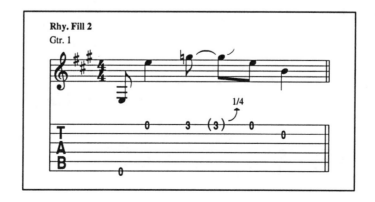

don't be   sur - prised   when they pull the wool   o - ver yo eyes. ___
bet - ter   get to it   in - stead ___ of just   stand - ing a - round. ___

Gtr. 4: Rhy. Fig. 1

Yeah, don't get funked up.
It's time to get down.

Come on, y'- all.
(Sing 2nd time only)

To Coda

1.
Gtr. 1: w/Riff A

Gtr. 4: w/Rhy. Fig. 1, (2 times)
Gtr. 1: w/Riff A, (8 times)

(Dah   doo dah,   dah   doo dah,   doo dah.)

w/slide

Oh, ___   yeah!   (Dah   doo dah,

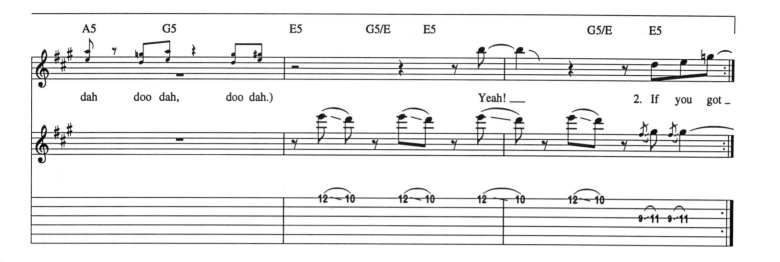

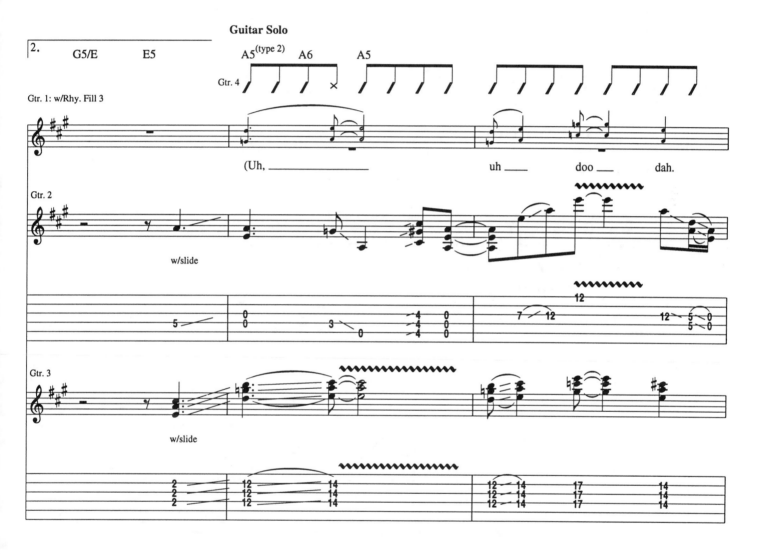

Dah doo dah, doo dah, doo dah, doo dah.

Dah doo dah, doo dah, doo dah, doo dah. Dah doo dah, doo

*Slide movement causes
3rd & 1st strings to sound.

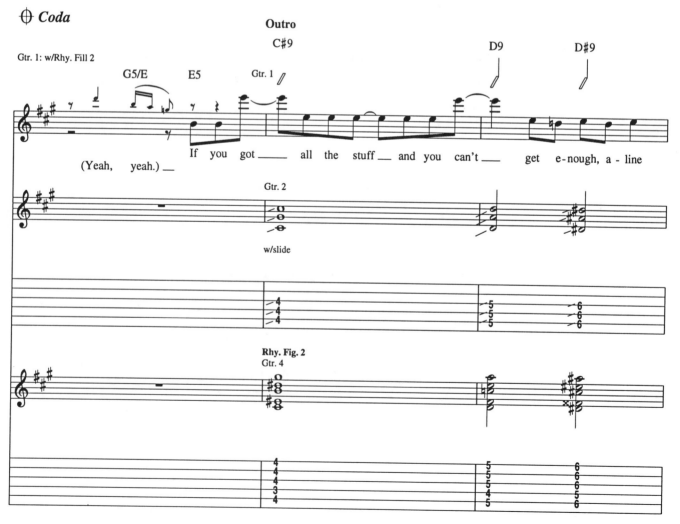

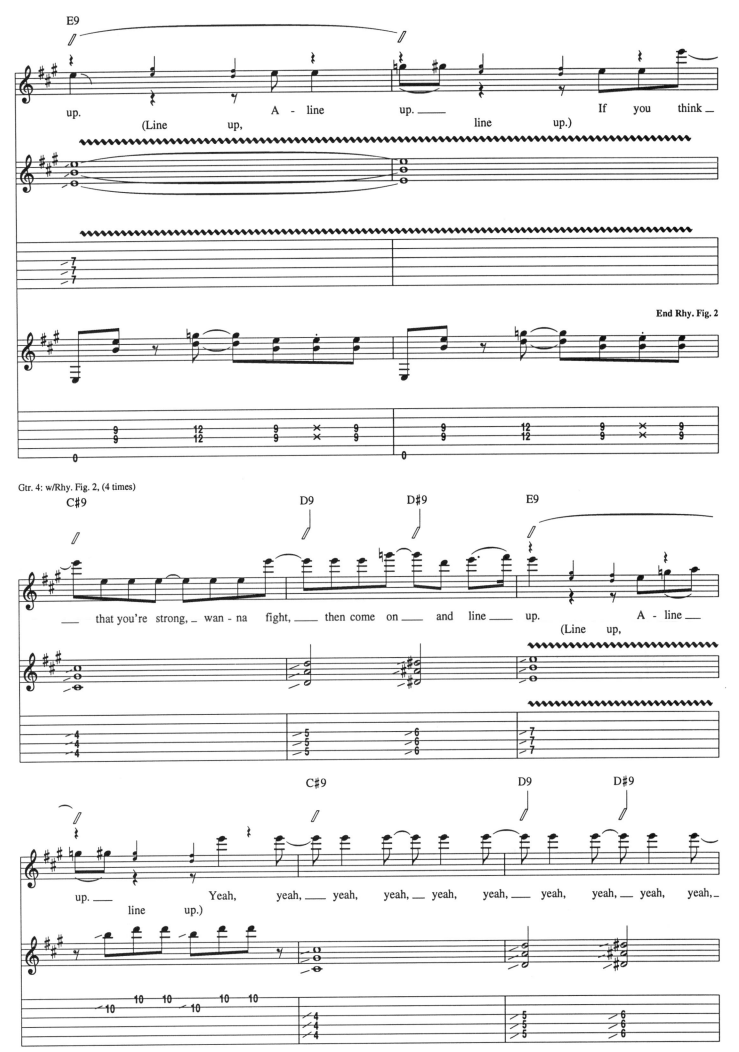

Amazing

Words and Music by Steven Tyler and Richie Supa

so sick and tired   of liv-in' a   lie. __   I was wish-in' that I__   would die. _____   It's a -

Chorus

maz   -   ing. __   with the   blink of an eye__   you fi-nal-ly see__   the light,

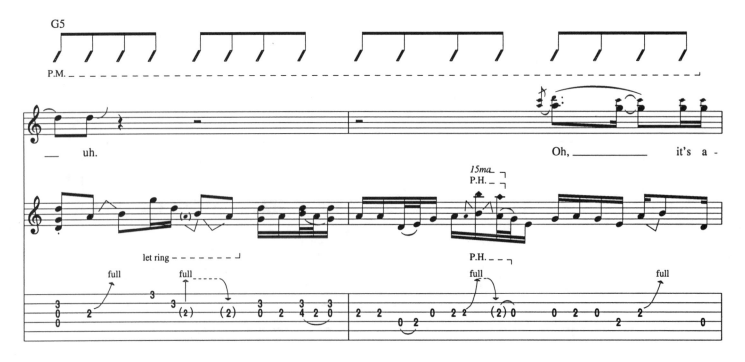

__ uh.   Oh, _____   it's a -

136

maz - ing, — when the mo-ment ar - rives ___ that you know you'll be ___ al -

right. Yeah, it's a -

maz - ing, and I'm say-in' a prayer ___ for the des-per-ate hearts ___ to - night.

Verse

Gtr. 1: w/Rhy. Fig. 1
Gtr. 4: w/Rhy. Fig. 2

learn to crawl, _ be - fore you learn to walk. _ But I

just could-n't lis - ten to all that right - eous talk. _____ Oh, yeah. _ Well, I was

w/Bkgd. Voc. Fig. 1

out on the street, _ just try - in' to sur - vive. _

Scratch - in' to stay _ a - live. _____ It's a -

Chorus

Gtr. 5

ma - zing, _____ with the blink of an eye _ you fi - nal - ly see - the light. _

Gtr. 4

let ring _ _ _ _ _ _   let ring _ _ _ _ _ _   let ring _ _ _ _ _ _   let ring _ _ _ _ _ _

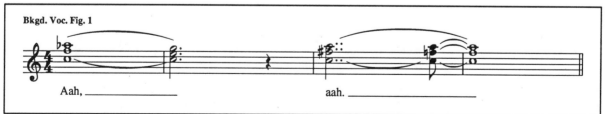

Bkgd. Voc. Fig. 1

Aah, _____ aah. _____

139

say-in' a prayer for the des-per-ate hearts to - night. The des-per-ate hearts, des-per-ate hearts.

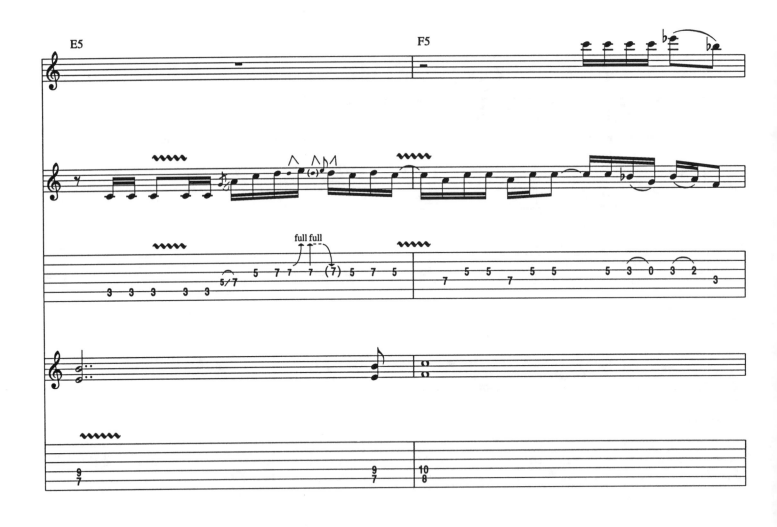

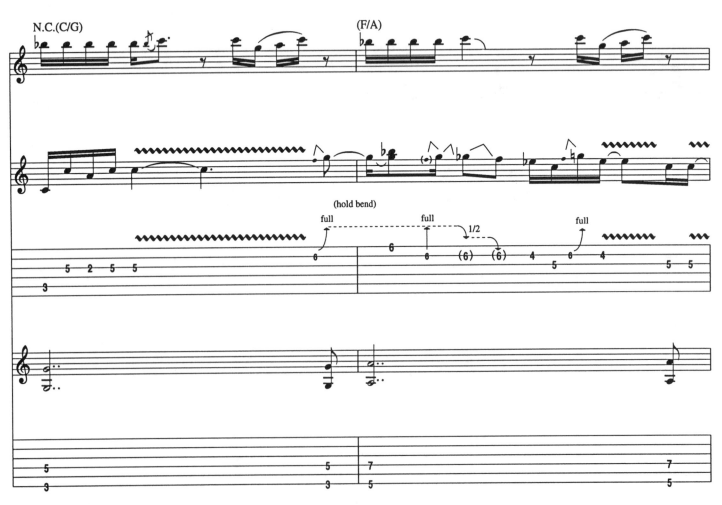

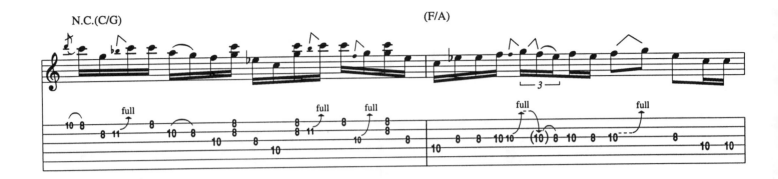

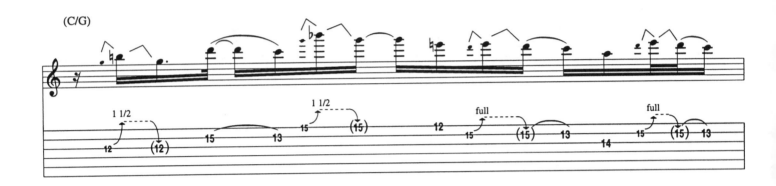

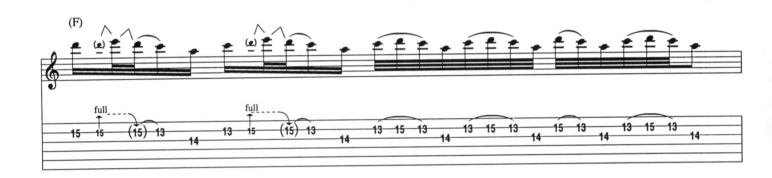

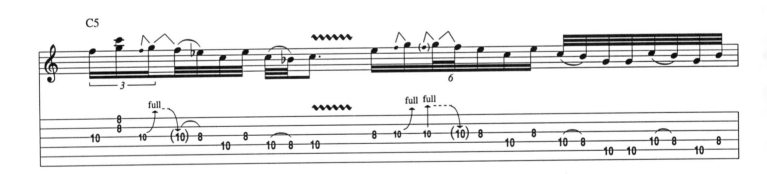

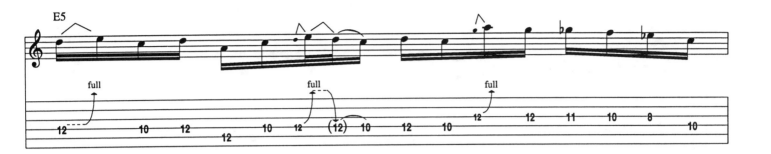

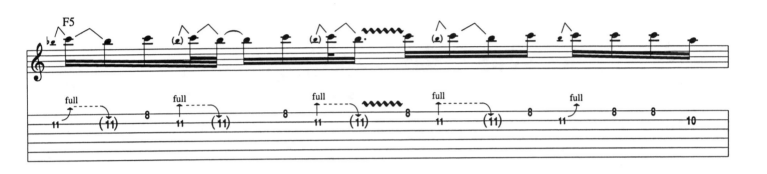

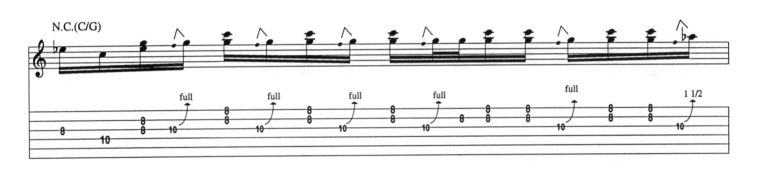

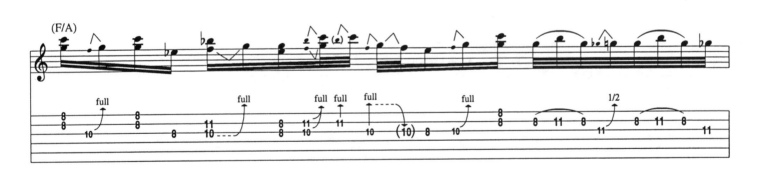

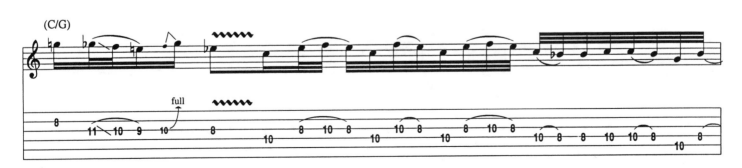

(F)

sounding pitches: G   G   A

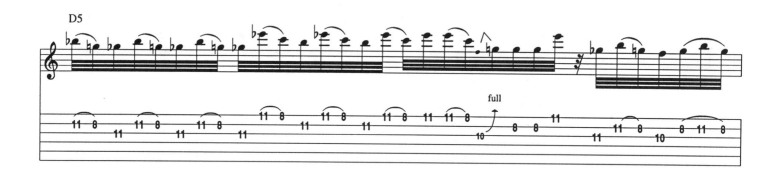

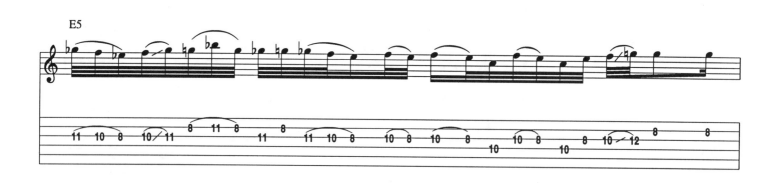

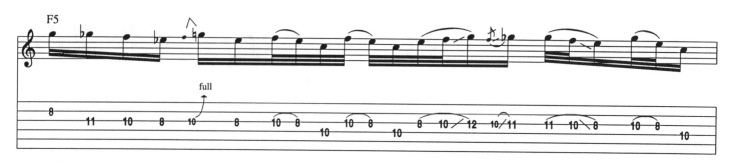

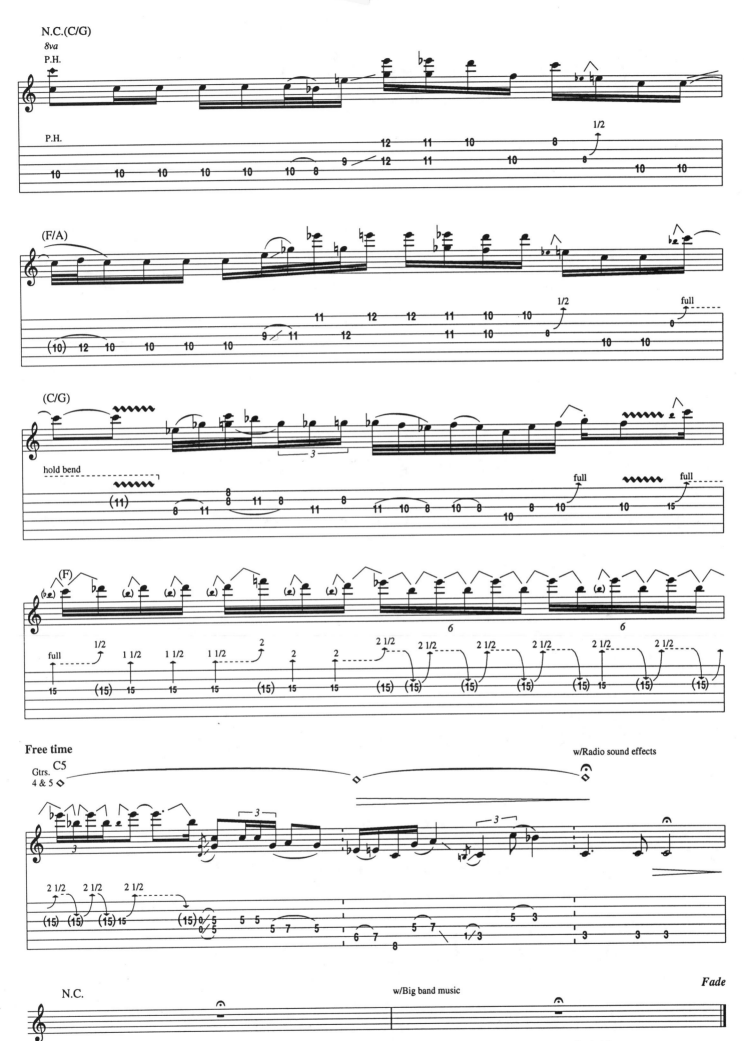

Spoken: So, from all of us in Aerosmith to all of you out there wherever you are.   Remember, the light at the end of the tunnel may be you. Good night.

Boogie Man

Words and Music by Steven Tyler and Joe Perry

*Some chord names implied by bass part.

NOTATION LEGEND

RECORDED VERSIONS

The Best Note-For-Note Transcriptions Available

BOOKS INCLUDE TABLATURE

2015 Aerosmith's Greatest Hits......................$18.95	00694894 Frank Gambale – The Great Explorers.....$18.95	00694868 Gary Moore – After Hours $18.95
0133 Aerosmith – Pump..............................$18.95	00694807 Danny Gatton – 88 Elmira St..................$17.95	00694849 Gary Moore – The Early Years.............$18.95
4865 Alice In Chains – Dirt $18.95	00694848 Genuine Rockabilly Guitar Hits................$19.95	00694872 Vinnie Moore – Meltdown.....................$18.95
0225 Alice In Chains – Facelift $18.95	00660326 Guitar Heroes $17.95	00694883 Nirvana – Nevermind...........................$18.95
4826 Anthrax – Attack Of The Killer B's...........$18.95	00694780 Guitar School Classics..........................$17.95	00694847 Ozzy Osbourne – The Best Of Ozzy..........$22.95
0227 Anthrax – Persistence Of Time.................$18.95	00694768 Guitar School Greatest Hits $17.95	00694830 Ozzy Osbourne – No More Tears...........$18.95
4797 Armored Saint – Symbol Of Salvation........$18.95	00694854 Buddy Guy – Damn Right,	00694855 Pearl Jam – Ten..............................$18.95
0051 Badlands $18.95	I've Got The Blues.........................$18.95	00693800 Pink Floyd – Early Classics $18.95
4863 Beatles – Sgt. Pepper's Lonely	00660325 The Harder Edge $17.95	00660188 Poison – Flesh & Blood......................$18.95
Hearts Club Band...........................$18.95	00694798 George Harrison Anthology....................$19.95	00693865 Poison – Look What The Cat Dragged In..$18.95
94832 Beatles – Acoustic Guitar Book...............$18.95	00692930 Jimi Hendrix-Are You Experienced?.........$19.95	00693864 The Best Of Police............................$18.95
94880 The Beatles – Abbey Road $18.95	00692931 Jimi Hendrix-Axis: Bold As Love............$19.95	00692535 Elvis Presley...................................$18.95
60140 The Beatles Guitar Book......................$18.95	00660192 The Jimi Hendrix Concerts....................$24.95	00693910 Ratt – Invasion of Your Privacy...............$18.95
94891 The Beatles – Revolver $18.95	00692932 Jimi Hendrix-Electric Ladyland $24.95	00693911 Ratt – Out Of The Cellar......................$18.95
94884 The Best of George Benson....................$19.95	00660099 Jimi Hendrix-Radio One $24.95	00660060 Robbie Robertson............................$18.95
92385 Chuck Berry $18.95	00660024 Jimi Hendrix-Variations On A Theme:	00694760 Rock Classics $17.95
92200 Black Sabbath – We Sold Our Soul	Red House.................................$18.95	00693474 Rock Superstars..............................$17.95
For Rock 'N' Roll...........................$18.95	00660029 Buddy Holly.................................$18.95	00694836 Richie Sambora – Stranger In This Town.$18.95
94821 Blue Heaven – Great Blues Guitar............$18.95	00660200 John Lee Hooker – The Healer $18.95	00694805 Scorpions – Crazy World $18.95
94770 Jon Bon Jovi – Blaze Of Glory.................$18.95	00660169 John Lee Hooker – A Blues Legend.........$17.95	00694885 Spin Doctors.................................$18.95
94871 Bon Jovi – Keep The Faith.....................$18.95	00694850 Iron Maiden – Fear Of The Dark $19.95	00694796 Steelheart....................................$18.95
94774 Bon Jovi – New Jersey.........................$18.95	00694761 Iron Maiden – No Prayer For The Dying..$18.95	00694180 Stryper – In God We Trust....................$18.95
94775 Bon Jovi – Slippery When Wet.................$18.95	00693096 Iron Maiden – Power Slave/	00694824 Best Of James Taylor.........................$14.95
94762 Cinderella – Heartbreak Station...............$18.95	Somewhere In Time........................$19.95	00694846 Testament – The Ritual.......................$18.95
92376 Cinderella – Long Cold Winter.................$18.95	00693095 Iron Maiden $22.95	00660084 Testament – Practice What You Preach ...$18.95
92375 Cinderella – Night Songs.......................$18.95	00694833 Billy Joel For Guitar $18.95	00694765 Testament – Souls Of Black $18.95
94869 Eric Clapton – Unplugged......................$18.95	00660147 Eric Johnson Guitar Transcriptions..........$18.95	00694887 Thin Lizzy – The Best Of Thin Lizzy..........$18.95
92392 Eric Clapton – Crossroads Vol. 1 ....$22.95	00694799 Robert Johnson – At The Crossroads $19.95	00694767 Trixter $18.95
92393 Eric Clapton – Crossroads Vol. 2 ....$22.95	00660226 Judas Priest – Painkiller $18.95	00694410 The Best of U2...............................$18.95
92394 Eric Clapton – Crossroads Vol. 3 ....$22.95	00693185 Judas Priest – Vintage Hits...................$18.95	00694411 U2 – The Joshua Tree........................$18.95
60139 Eric Clapton – Journeyman....................$18.95	00693186 Judas Priest – Metal Cuts....................$18.95	00660137 Steve Vai – Passion & Warfare $24.95
92391 The Best of Eric Clapton $18.95	00693187 Judas Priest – Ram It Down..................$18.95	00694879 Stevie Ray Vaughan – In The Beginning ...$18.95
694896 John Mayall/Eric Clapton – Bluesbreakers..$18.95	00694764 Kentucky Headhunters –	00660136 Stevie Ray Vaughan – In Step $18.95
694873 Eric Clapton – Timepieces....................$18.95	Pickin' On Nashville........................$18.95	00660058 Stevie Ray Vaughan –
694788 Classic Rock....................................$17.95	00694795 Kentucky Headhunters – Electric Barnyard.$18.95	Lightnin' Blues 1983 – 1987 ....$22.95
694793 Classic Rock Instrumentals....................$16.95	00660050 B. B. King $18.95	00694835 Stevie Ray Vaughan – The Sky Is Crying ..$18.95
694862 Contemporary Country Guitar $18.95	00660068 Kix – Blow My Fuse $18.95	00694776 Vaughan Brothers – Family Style.............$18.95
660127 Alice Cooper – Trash...........................$18.95	00694806 L.A. Guns – Hollywood Vampires............$18.95	00660196 Vixen – Rev It Up.............................$18.95
694840 Cream – Disraeli Gears.........................$14.95	00694794 Best Of Los Lobos $18.95	00660054 W.A.S.P. – The Headless Children...........$18.95
694844 Def Leppard – Adrenalize.....................$18.95	00660199 The Lynch Mob – Wicked Sensation $18.95	00694787 Warrant – Dirty Rotten Filthy Stinking Rich.$18.95
692440 Def Leppard – High 'N' Dry/Pyromania....$18.95	00693412 Lynyrd Skynyrd $18.95	00694866 Warrant – Dog Eat Dog......................$18.95
692430 Def Leppard – Hysteria........................$18.95	00660174 Yngwie Malmsteen – Eclipse..................$18.95	00694781 Warrant – Cherry Pie........................$18.95
660186 Alex De Grassi Guitar Collection $16.95	00694845 Yngwie Malmsteen – Fire And Ice............$18.95	00694786 Winger.......................................$18.95
694831 Derek And The Dominos – Layla & Other	00694756 Yngwie Malmsteen – Marching Out $18.95	00694782 Winger – In The Heart Of The Young.......$18.95
Assorted Love Songs $19.95	00694755 Yngwie Malmsteen's Rising Force $18.95	
692240 Bo Diddley Guitar Solos.......................$18.95	00660001 Yngwie Malmsteen Rising Force – Odyssey.$18.95	
660175 Dio – Lock Up The Wolves....................$18.95	00694757 Yngwie Malmsteen – Trilogy...................$18.95	
660178 Willie Dixon.....................................$24.95	00692880 Metal Madness................................$17.95	
694800 FireHouse $18.95	00694792 Metal Church – The Human Factor..........$18.95	
694867 FireHouse – Hold Your Fire...................$18.95	00660229 Monster Metal Ballads $19.95	
660184 Lita Ford – Stiletto $18.95	00694802 Gary Moore – Still Got The Blues.............$18.95	

0993